I0460168

A BEAUTIFUL CAT STORY

What Happened After the First Meow

Becky Divinski

BCD COMMUNICATIONS
PUBLISHING

BCD Communications Publishing

Copyright © 2024 by Becky Divinski

All rights reserved.

No portion of this book may be reproduced in any form without written permission from the publisher or author except as permitted by U.S. copyright law.

For privacy reasons, some names and characteristics have been changed.

This publication is designed to provide accurate and authoritative information regarding the subject matter covered. It is sold with the understanding that neither the author nor the publisher is engaged in rendering professional services related to the subject matter. While the publisher and author have used their best efforts in preparing this book, they make no representations or warranties with respect to the accuracy or completeness of the contents of this book and specifically disclaim any implied warranties of merchantability or fitness for a particular purpose. The advice and strategies contained herein may not be suitable for your situation. You should consult with a veterinary professional in matters relating to a cat's health or behavior, particularly with respect to any symptoms that may require diagnosis or medical attention when appropriate. Neither the publisher nor the author shall be liable for any loss of profit or other commercial damages, including but not limited to special, incidental, consequential, personal, or other damages.

While the author has made every effort to provide accurate Internet addresses at the time of publication, neither the publisher nor the author assumes any responsibility for errors or changes after publication. Also, the author and publisher do not have any control over nor assume any responsibility for third-party websites or their content.

Book Cover by Angie Alaya

First edition 2024

Printed in the United States of America

Paperback ISBN: 979-8-9913679-0-5

Ebook ISBN: 979-8-9913679-1-2

Dedication

This beautiful cat story is dedicated to one of the most beautiful cats I've known, Mr. Pumpkin. Although he is gone—Mr. Pumpkin passed years before this beautiful cat story—he is not forgotten. I will forever be grateful to Mr. Pumpkin for being an excellent "trainer cat" whose patience with my daughter helped her as she learned to care for cats. Mr. Pumpkin had a big heart and gave the best hugs.

*Mr. Pumpkin and his
sister Calli napping*

Contents

Introduction

One month before the story in this book occurred, I did a favor for one of my friends. He asked me to stay at his home while he was away on vacation and care for the colony of 10 outdoor cats that had taken up residence there (His local animal care organization is small, so there are many community cats in his area.) This opportunity helped me understand community cats more—how they would eat the food *after* I walked away. Also, only the kittens and a few other cats who had been around humans would let me pet them.

On my flight home, I reflected on that cat-sitting experience. It led me to think about the future, and I knew I wanted to volunteer somewhere when I had more time. My criteria for volunteering were that it needed to be something I enjoyed and could connect with personally.

I thought about my love of cats and how interconnected my life has been with cats over the years, starting when I was a baby with our cat, Fluffy. Later, as a kindergartener, I had an opportunity to play with a litter of kittens, and that time with the kittens left a lasting impression on me.

I considered that it might be fun to volunteer to foster kittens someday, which would help the community at the same time. I knew that fostering kittens required time and work and needed to be done in another part of my house, away from my family's three cats. Again, these were just my thoughts, and it was something I wished for at a later date. I didn't have the time or energy to volunteer then. My advice: "Be careful what you wish for." As you read this book, you'll understand what I mean.

I learned a lot from the experiences you'll read about in this book. The poet Maya Angelou expressed learning from one's experiences so beautifully with these words, "I did then what I knew how to do. Now that I know better, I do better." By sharing these experiences with you, I feel like I'm helping you to know better so you can do better by avoiding some of the pitfalls I encountered. To do this, I've scattered cat facts and tips throughout the book so you, too, can gain more cat wisdom.

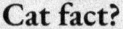
Cat fact?
This questioning cat identifies a learning segment about cats. *{References ...}*

Cat tip:
This light bulb with the cat paw identifies a helpful hint on a cat topic. *{References ...}*

The formula for *{References ...}*, where *References* is the References section near the back of this book, is:

- *{References: Books: <number>, pg(s).<page number(s)>}*

  ◦ *<number>* identifies the listing in the Books area

  ◦ *<page number(s)>* identifies the page or pages within the book where the information can be found

- *{References: Websites: <number><letter>}*

  ◦ *<number>* identifies the listing in the Websites area

  ◦ *<letter>* identifies specific information within the website and its URL

I had two big motivations for writing this book. First, it is a special story that I want to share with people, which will keep this wonderful experience alive. Second, you'll read about this motivation in the Afterword. It will make more sense after you've read the story.

This beautiful cat story is a journey full of twists and turns. Enjoy!

A Little Surprise

"Hey, do you hear that?" These words, spoken by my husband on a sunny Saturday afternoon, changed the trajectory of our lives for the next five months. Who knew that the actions following those simple words would start my family on a journey filled with numerous decisions to make? Little did I know that this journey, at times, would stretch me to my limits, both physically and emotionally. The 19th-century German philosopher Friedrich Nietzsche's words, "What doesn't kill you makes you stronger," applied to my part of this journey.

Earlier that day, my husband and I picked up our daughter, Christina, from the airport. Having recently completed her second year in college, she traveled across the country that day to get home. After a short stay, she would then travel to her summer school program. I almost didn't recognize her, my own daughter! Christina looked burned out after a hectic few days of finals, packing up her apartment and moving her belongings into a storage unit for the summer.

After arriving home, Christina greeted our three cats, tightly hugging Ella, her favorite. Christina announced, "I want to take Ella to college with me in the fall." I replied, "It wouldn't be fair to her sister, Leia. Those two are tightly bonded." Ella, a gray tabby, and Leia, a white and black cow cat, had spent all their five years together. I mentioned to Christina, "You can take both cats when the timing is right for your living situation." That would leave my husband and I with Calli, the 12-year-old orange, black, and white calico cat who wants to be the "only" cat, having all of our attention.

Christina agreed and moved on. Before dragging herself off to take a much-needed nap, Christina wistfully commented, "I wish I had a kitten to take back to college." While smiling, I responded, "I understand how you feel because kittens are so cute and cuddly." With Christina's busy college life, having a kitten was a fun idea, not a practical reality.

During Christina's nap, my husband followed his usual Saturday routine by working on projects in his "man cave," aka garage. I enjoyed the sunny weather while trimming the rosemary bush in the backyard. When I took a break and walked towards him, he motioned me over to the edge of the garage. That's when he uttered those fateful words, "Hey, do you hear that?" He followed that up with, "It sounds like a cat." I heard the sound, too, and became concerned, thinking one of our three indoor cats had gotten out. Then, I heard the sound again and said, "Oh, yeah, I hear it, but it's a young meow. I think it's a kitten." He replied, "Wow, there must be a kitten o ver there."

I walked over to where the meow came from, the narrow space between our garage and a neighbor's fence. This space measured about one foot wide between the garage and the fence and about 20 feet long from front to back. The problem was getting closer to the space to take a better look. Two possible options were the front access, near the front of the garage where my husband and I stood, and the back access, near the back of the garage.

A wild blackberry bush with sharp thorns on its twisted branches menacingly covered this back access to the space. I couldn't get close enough to take a look and wasn't in the mood to take on the blackberry bush that day. Recently, I lost a battle with the bush when I began trimming it back. Wearing a long-sleeved shirt hadn't helped. My arms sustained injuries from thorn cuts.

That left me with the other option—the front access to the space. This access point required someone to squeeze between the front of the garage and a small, heavy shed less than nine inches apart. That disqualified my husband. Unfortunately, that left me and my daughter, who was still asleep. I didn't want to wait. With my left hand gripping the garage opening, I squeezed into the tight space and, like a contortionist, leaned over to the right to take a look. I steadied myself with my right hand on top of the two 4-foot-tall boards in front of the opening.

As I peered in, I noticed the space had a layer of dirt as its floor. Leftover, neatly stacked house siding filled up about half of the space. About five feet from where I stood, the siding extended from there to the back of the space. A 4-foot-tall roll of green plastic fencing stood upright against the 4-foot-tall boards. A big round attic fan leaned against the plastic fencing.

As I continued taking in the scene, I heard a little meow. It came from underneath the plastic fencing. As I reached over to lift the fencing, I heard hissing nearby. I turned my head and saw a cat about five feet in front of me, sitting on top of the siding. This cat seemed to appear out of nowhere. I assumed it was the mother cat sending me a warning. I decided to give her some space and squeezed myself back out to the driveway. I told my husband, "Let's wait until the cat leaves to get some food, and then I can peek at her kitten and check out the situation more."

In the meantime, I contacted our friend, Tonya, who had previously fostered young kittens, bottle-feeding them every two hours for several weeks. She did this for two local animal welfare organizations. Tonya would know what to do. I texted her, "Since you've dealt with kittens—What should we do with a mother cat and her one or more kittens? We hear at least one kitten meowing next to our garage. When I investigated, I saw the mother cat, and she hissed at me. We can't get to the kitten easily, but it's probably protected from other animals."

About two hours after meeting the mother cat, I saw her leave the space. She walked on top of the 6-foot-tall fence bordering the space. Fortunately, I had visibility from my kitchen window to that part of the fence and saw her leave my backyard. I waited a short time and then went to the space to see the kitten. I grabbed the top of the plastic fencing roll, lifting it slightly off the ground for a look. Lo and behold, the one kitten was actually five kittens! They were so cute, fluffy, and small! With open eyes, they climbed over each other like wiggly worms. The kitten litter consisted of two orange tabbies, two gray tabbies, and one black-and-white tuxedo.

What's the average size of a cat litter? 4-6 kittens. The mother cat's age, health, and breed affect the litter's size. The largest litter of domestic cats on record was 19 kittens in 1970 in the UK. *{References: Websites: 1a, 2a}*

I pondered, "A mother cat and five kittens are in our backyard. Now, what do I do? How do I take care of them?" Our household already had three cats, and I felt concerned about the forecasted rain. Should I consider taking the kittens into the house now? I didn't know their health situation. Could they have any diseases that could spread to our cats? Was the mother cat feral[1] ? How would we catch her and handle her in the house if we did manage to catch her?

I wondered whether the mother cat had moved the kittens into the space or if they had been born there. It would remain a mystery for now. Suspecting the mother cat would return soon, I restored the fencing roll to its original spot and returned to my gardening.

Soon after, Christina woke up from her nap, and my husband and I told her what had happened. She, of course, wanted to see the kittens. The mother cat hadn't returned, so Christina and I went into stealth mode, snapping pictures and recording video before carefully replacing the fencing roll over the kittens. I reminded Christina that she had wished for a kitten to take back to college. I asked her not to wish for things like this again. Apparently, Christina possesses special powers. Instead of one kitten—voilà—five kittens appeared within hours! If only she had used her wish towards college tuition!

Next, we connected with Tonya by phone. She asked for the age of the kittens. We weren't sure, so she pointed us to the "Kitten Lady" website, which provides a wealth of information on kittens, including how to determine a kitten's age. I compared our backyard kittens to those on the kitten age webpage. Although our backyard kittens' ears looked unfolded, I

---

1. An unowned, outdoor cat who isn't socialized, meaning it's not used to being around people. *{References: Websites: 3a}*

wasn't sure they were three weeks old yet. We guessed that they were between two and three weeks old.

How do I determine a kitten's age? Some factors to consider are: Is the umbilical cord attached? Are the eyes open? Are the ears folded? Are they walking wobbly? The "Kitten Lady" website has a good chart to help determine a kitten's age. *{References: Websites: 4a}*

Tonya provided us with a list of places that took in kittens, including where she had volunteered. I intended to contact these places and pass along the mother cat and kittens to one of them. I assumed a place that could take the mother cat and kittens would socialize them all before adopting them out.

The next day, when I peeked around the corner to see if the mother cat was there, she hissed. Her hisses effectively kept me at a distance. I considered her a good and protective mother cat for her kittens.

Wanting better visibility to the kittens, I took my chances with the blackberry bush, cutting it back and peering through the back access to the space. It didn't help—I couldn't see the kittens. Christina and I rushed to a nearby store to buy an inexpensive camera before it closed. We'd use it to observe the cat action in the space from a distance, using the camera's app on our phones. That way, we would avoid bothering the mother cat.

The following day, I contacted my friend Karen, whose daughter, Daria, worked at a veterinary hospital. I wanted Daria's advice about taking the kittens inside or not. I had heard that the next two days would be rainy, and I was concerned that the ground near the kittens might get wet. The problem was that the garage roof above the kittens' space was only a short overhang that didn't completely cover that space.

Karen relayed Daria's advice, "If the mom isn't taking care of the kittens, then you can take them inside your house or garage, and you would have to either take care of them, i.e., feed them, or get them to the shelter so that they get fed. If the mom cat is caring for them, it's probably better to leave them where they are. Still, if you don't want to have five more feral cats in your neighborhood, you should eventually take them to the shelter and maybe ask the shelter what they recommend regarding when to bring them in. Also, giving the nursing momma cat kitten food is good."

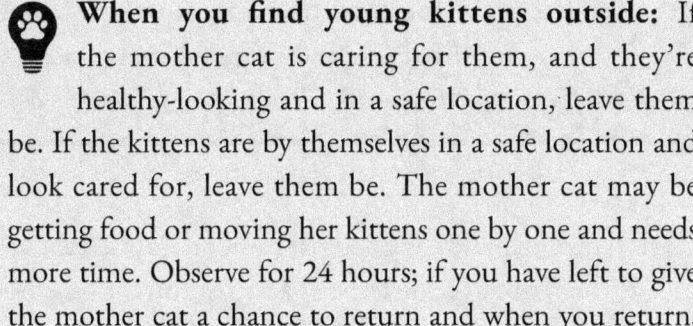

When you find young kittens outside: If the mother cat is caring for them, and they're healthy-looking and in a safe location, leave them be. If the kittens are by themselves in a safe location and look cared for, leave them be. The mother cat may be getting food or moving her kittens one by one and needs more time. Observe for 24 hours; if you have left to give the mother cat a chance to return and when you return, she hasn't, and the kittens look sick and are crying, it's time to help the kittens (They need to be bottle-fed and stimulated to pee/poop after they are fed. The mother cat typically does this.) *{References: Websites: 5a}*

I appreciated Daria's helpful information. I felt relief knowing that the best course of action in this case was to leave the care of the kittens to their mother cat and leave food and water out for her. Daria's reference to the mother cat as a momma cat stuck with me. I thought that giving the generic name Momma Cat would keep me from becoming too attached to her. I imagined she would be someone else's cat someday. Then, she'd receive a specific name that matched her personality or appearance.

Feed kitten food to nursing mother cats: Nursing mother cats need more fat and protein, typically in kitten food. *{References: Websites: 4b}*

That day, my husband installed the camera, dubbed the "cat cam," at the front access to the space. I wanted to see how often Momma Cat returned to feed her kittens. As far as I could tell, the kittens looked and sounded healthy—they weren't meowing a lot.

The cat cam worked well for our purposes, except for the light, which came on at night and attracted bugs. The price was right (only $35); it had been in stock at the store, and it was listed as an indoor camera, so I couldn't complain. Since the cat cam recorded movement, we had many videos of bugs going after the camera light. Fortunately, we also got many videos of Momma Cat entering and exiting the s pace.

As luck would have it, the very next day, someone from one of the local animal welfare organizations, Sage, posted a message on an online community bulletin board that I'm on. She was looking for a family to foster a mother cat and her kittens. After reading Sage's message, I decided to contact her for advice about my mother cat and kitten situation. I planned to wait a few days to give Sage a chance to deal with responses to her message. Also, I wanted more time to check out other cat resources I had been given.

Hopefully, soon, I could pass Momma Cat and her kittens along to a caring organization. This situation was new to me, and I wanted to take the right steps for their care. Also, my life had gotten busier before they arrived, so my time was more limited. Tomorrow, I will ask Christina for help sorting out the possible cat resource places for Momma Cat and the kittens.

An Unexpected Move

While I ran errands the next morning, Christina went to the space to check out the kittens. She texted me, "The kittens are very noisy." I told her, "I'll look in on them when I return." I suspected Momma Cat was temporarily gone, and her kittens were hungry.

When I returned from running errands, I checked on the kittens. What happened was a scenario I hadn't considered—Momma Cat moving the kittens. I couldn't believe that all the kittens were gone! She moved them during the 75-minute period between when Christina viewed the kittens and when I returned home. I wonder if Momma Cat saw Christina looking at the kittens. On the other hand, maybe it had nothing to do with Christina, but Momma Cat instinctively felt it was time to move her kittens.

Why does a mother cat move her kittens?
When she feels the nest[1] is no longer safe, there's too much human interest, too much noise or light, a dirty nest, or at least one sick kitten, it's time to relocate. *{References: Websites: 1b}*

Moving the five kittens probably required Momma Cat to get some cooperation from her kittens. It would have made it easier for her if the five kittens crawled out from underneath the rolled fencing—something the kittens could have done at their age. Since the kittens were too little to jump high, a requirement for the next part of their move, Momma Cat would need to pick them up one at a time by their scruff[2] while she completed the next step. During this step, Momma Cat had three paths to choose from. The first path: jump up onto the siding, walk to the back of the space, and then jump down off the siding. This required her to walk close to the thorny blackberry bush to get to the backyard area behind the

---

1. The bed/space for kittens. *{Resources: Websites: 6a}*

2. The loose skin at the back of a cat's neck. *{References: Websites: 1c}*

garage. The second path: jump up onto the siding, jump up onto the narrow fence, and jump down into the neighbor's backyard. The third path: jump up and over two tall boards leaning against each other, then land in the narrow driveway area between the garage and small shed.

I had a feeling Momma Cat moved her kittens close by. I guessed that she took the first path leading to a grassy area behind the garage. Moving quickly and quietly, I checked that area for the kittens. Bingo—I found them! Momma Cat moved them into a more accessible location for her to get into. I also found it more accessible for my family to view the kittens. Large boards lay at an angle against the back of the garage, with long rectangular boards leaning against each other on the ground, serving as a "running pen" boundary for the kittens. There was an open space in the middle of the "running pen" where we could see the kittens. However, there were drawbacks to this space. The openings in the middle and at both ends left the kittens exposed to other animals. Also, the little overhang from the garage roof stopped short of shielding the middle opening of the space from rain.

I noticed Momma Cat was away from her kittens, so I took a closer look at them. I saw four kittens huddled together in a pile. The fifth kitten, an orange tabby, was missing. Maybe Momma Cat was in the process of moving it. Even though I could easily have petted the four kittens—they looked cute—I refrained and took off before Momma Cat saw me. I wanted to avoid Momma Cat getting spooked and moving her kittens yet again.

My concern about other animals bothering the kittens was valid. Over the years, various animal visitors have been in my backyard, including raccoons, skunks, possums, squirrels, rats, and other cats. My other concern was the weather, which had turned cold. It had started raining and continued off and on throughout the rest of that day.

Did I need to take the kittens inside our house and care for them? I continued observing the situation via the cat cam, which my husband moved to capture the latest happenings at the newest kitten location. I hoped Momma Cat would move them to a more covered and still accessible location soon.

When I checked on the kittens later that day, I felt relieved to see the missing orange kitten with the rest of the litter. I decided to have faith in Momma Cat to protect her kittens from other animals and the rain. I left them and went inside the house.

Over the next several days, I worked on building trust with Momma Cat. Luckily, my recent experience caring for my friend's colony of 10 outdoor, primarily feral cats, helped prepare me for this. I learned to give the cats more space and to move slowly to avoid startling them. Feral cats generally don't trust people. The key to building trust with feral cats—feed them.

I began feeding Momma Cat twice a day. At each feeding, I put out a bowl of water and a bowl filled halfway each with wet and dry food. Since it had been raining, I used a plastic bin on its side to serve as an umbrella over the bowls. When it wasn't raining, the ants posed a problem, so after Momma Cat ate, I removed the food bowl.

After a few days, Momma Cat and I fell into a shared morning routine. She waited for me, sitting at an easy-to-escape distance from the back door of my house. When I exited the house, she ran but remained in the yard. After I put the food and water down, she waited until I walked about 20 feet away before wandering over to devour her meal.

This was my first experience with a feral mother cat and her kittens. I needed help. After checking out other cat resources, I sent Sage a message. Since she was associated with a local animal welfare organization, I felt she could point me in the right direction for help.

Help is on the Way

S age replied to my email, and we scheduled a time to talk. I felt relieved to know I could ask her questions—I had a lot! I assumed Momma Cat was feral because she hissed a lot when I came within 20 feet of her or the kittens.

When Sage and I spoke, she said that Momma Cat was probably a feral or community cat[1]. This meant that Momma Cat probably wouldn't be adoptable and would need to remain outside. How did I feel about having an outside cat? Since I had fed her regularly, she might decide to stay in my backyard. Why would she want to leave when she had her meals covered?

---

1. An unowned cat who lives outdoors. *{References: Web-sites: 3a}*

I described Momma Cat to Sage as a beautiful orange, black, and white calico cat, probably less than one-year-old—a kitten herself. Momma Cat often stood with her four paws together, which made her look bigger. Maybe that was her goal.

When do kittens become adult cats? Most cats are considered kittens until they turn one year old. Some longhaired breeds are exceptions and can develop even to five years old. *{References: Websites: 1d}*

Sage and I discussed the following steps for moving forward with Momma Cat and the kittens:

Step 1: Leave the kittens outside with Momma Cat until they are about five weeks old, the average age at which most kittens are weaned.

Step 2: Trap Momma Cat.

Step 3: Round up the kittens and bring them inside the house.

Step 4: Take Momma Cat in for spay surgery.

What does it mean to spay or neuter a cat? Both are surgical procedures to remove a cat's reproductive parts (also known as sterilization). A spay surgery is performed on a female cat (queen[2]), and neuter surgery is performed on a male cat(tom[3]). *{References: Books: 2, pgs.174-175}*

Step 5: After surgery, bring Momma Cat back to my house to heal and finish weaning her kittens if she hasn't already done so.

Step 6: When kittens are weaned, release Momma Cat outside to rejoin her feral cat community.

Step 7: Find an animal welfare organization to take the kittens. The organization could find someone to foster them until the kittens reached eight weeks old and weighed about two pounds. They would then be prepared for adoption, which included having spay/neuter surgeries and receiving vaccinations.

---

2. A female cat that hasn't been spayed. *{References: Websites: 6b}*

3. A male cat that hasn't been neutered. *{References: Websites: 6c}*

Sage explained that many local animal welfare organizations were at capacity[4]. During the pandemic, people couldn't turn cats into organizations like before, so the cat population substantially increased. Since it was kitten season, they were now seeing the effects.

> **When is kitten season?** Kitten season varies depending on whether it's a warm climate or not. In the Northern Hemisphere, kitten season typically runs from January through late fall. For example, California's kitten season typically runs from March through October. In some places in the world, kitten season is all year round. *{References: Websites: 1e}*

After this discussion, I researched some on my own and discovered that male cats can start fathering kittens at six months old. The average age at which female cats can start having kittens is six months old. However, some can begin as early as four months old. The typical gestation[5] period for cats is

---

4. Dealing with the largest possible number or amount. *{References: Websites: 6d}*

5. the carrying of young in the uterus; pregnancy *{References: Websites: 6e}*

60-65 days. Cats can have 2-3 litters of kittens in one year.[6] The average size of a litter is between 4-6 kittens. One potential scenario of exponential cat population growth is: "A single un-spayed female cat, and her offspring, can theoretically produce as many as 350,000 kittens in just 7 years[7]."

That's a lot of kittens! I reflected on Sage's comment about animal welfare organizations being at capacity and not having enough space for kittens. I asked her what was involved in fostering the kittens. After Sage laid out the responsibilities of being a kitten foster parent, I decided to keep an open mind and consider fostering the kittens myself.

Several days passed, and the time arrived for Christina to leave for her summer program. Christina and I talked about her petting a kitten that morning before leaving for the airport. I agreed with her plan as long as Momma Cat wasn't around. We didn't see Momma Cat, so Christina petted one of the orange tabby kittens. It seemed harmless enough because they were about four weeks old. It would be Christina's last chance to see them.

The loud hissing from the nearby blackberry bush suddenly jolted us out of our kitten bliss. When I peeked into the bush, I discovered Momma Cat inside, and she was NOT happy! Her tensed body, back hunched, and ears pulled tightly back told

---

6. {References: Websites: 1f}

7. {References: Websites: 1g}

us we had crossed a line with her. Christina quickly placed the kitten back into the nest, and we hurried into the house.

After dropping Christina off at the airport, my husband and I returned home, and I checked on the kittens. They were gone! Momma Cat moved them again! I had a sneaky suspicion about where she moved them. Luckily, I saw Momma Cat checking out the garden shed near the back fence a few days before. She had walked around the shed and looked underneath, too. I now suspected she had moved the kittens there.

Sure enough, while pruning roses in the backyard that afternoon, I spotted Momma Cat walking behind the shed. Soon after, I heard kittens meowing. I walked closer to the shed, and Momma Cat appeared from behind it. Then, I heard a little meow coming from underneath the shed. I realized Momma Cat had dropped her kittens into the squirrel tunnels under that shed. I lamented to myself, "Great! Capturing the kittens will be much harder now after Momma Cat is trapped."

Later that day, I picked up the cat trap and supplies from Sage. With my husband's help, I practiced setting up the trap inside our garage that evening. On the official trapping day, I hoped the trap wouldn't get set off too soon, for example, if Momma Cat bumped into it when walking inside. The trap bar seemed pretty sensitive. I probably worried more because it was my first time trapping a cat.

The following day, Momma Cat sat atop a wood pile near the garden shed, protecting her new nest like a lioness. She disappeared behind the shed when I brought out her food and water. Later that morning, I saw a squirrel standing where Momma Cat had been sitting earlier. I thought, "Oh, no, the squirrel and Momma Cat might fight because she uses the squirrel tunnels for her kittens." Usually, the cat would win in a cat vs. squirrel fight; however, this was a BIG squirrel, so I had doubts about Momma Cat coming out as the victor in this scenario. Then again, she was a mother cat and likely would protect her kittens at all costs.

About an hour later, I went outside to change Momma Cat's food and water. Since the recent nest move, I relocated the food and water bowls closer to the shed. I took a peek behind the shed to see if any kittens had come out from underneath. I found Momma Cat lying on the ground, nursing two of her kittens. I quietly backed up and sat nearby, still able to see them. I noticed the kittens lying on their bellies while nursing.

> **Why is it important that kittens lie on their bellies when nursing?** *This is to avoid getting fluid in their lungs. For this same reason, kittens should be on their bellies when bottle-fed. {References: Websites: 1h}*

I felt at peace watching Momma Cat nurse her kittens. It seemed like I was witnessing a special moment in time. I didn't want Momma Cat to catch me watching them, though. I thought it might cause her to be protective of her kittens and lose some trust in me. Also, I wanted to help the kittens get their entire meal. However, I didn't want them to hear me get up, so I took my chances and stayed put until Momma Cat finished nursing them. Then, I quietly got up and went back into my house.

On the Move—Again?!

Early that afternoon, I became anxious while look-ing out the family room window into my backyard. Momma Cat walked along the fence between my and a neighbor's backyard. I imagined she looked at my neigh-bor's backyard to size it up as a potential location to move her kittens.

We needed to move trap operations up a few days since Mom-ma Cat appeared to be gearing up to make a move. However, before trapping her, I needed to know where her kittens were, and her frequent nest moves made it more difficult for me. I had hoped she would become more comfortable with me and not move the kittens again. Also, there could be other reasons why she might want to move the kittens from under the shed (squirrel problems, perhaps?).

I regretted not grabbing the kittens the prior day when they were still easily accessible behind the garage. I asked Sage, "Should I consider grabbing the kittens before Momma Cat moves them again and then work on trapping her soon after? It's hard to know because the kittens still seem dependent on her for food. I haven't seen her bring them to the food or water bowls yet."

Sage reminded me that we needed to trap Momma Cat first, and probably the sooner, the better. Momma Cat had a TNR appointment on Tuesday. I needed to trap her on Sunday or Monday. Since Sunday was Mother's Day, I opted to trap her on Monday.

> **What is TNR?** TNR stands for Trap-Neuter-Return. A feral cat is first trapped, next neutered or spayed, and finally returned to its original location. Cats often have an ear tip (a small notch in the top of one ear) to signify they underwent the TNR process. *{References: Websites: 3b}*

I talked with my neighbor to give him a heads-up about the situation and share my concerns.

I told him, "A cat, probably a type of calico—white with orange and black coloring—has been walking on the fence between our two backyards a lot lately. She has five kittens and moved them to a new spot under my garden shed in the abandoned squirrel tunnels. I suspect she will move them again soon, as she has been eyeing locations in your backyard. Someone from one of the local animal care organizations is coaching me on trapping the feral mother cat and her kittens. I plan to trap her on Monday."

He mentioned seeing the mother cat in his backyard a few days ago.

Shortly afterward, I saw Momma Cat leave my backyard. Given this opportunity, I peered under the garden shed with my flashlight. It wasn't easy to see, and I barely spotted the orange kitten near the opening. I heard a sound like coughing. This nest concerned me because it only consisted of dirt. Also, only hearing one kitten left me wondering if Momma Cat had already moved the other kittens into my neighbor's backyard.

Later that day, while working inside, near the front of my house, I heard a kitten meowing. I went outside to investigate where the meow came from. I began searching in the front yard. A small gate nearby opened into the backyard, and I realized that Momma Cat might eventually try to move the kittens out of my yard by going underneath that gate. I began filling spaces underneath the gate with bricks. Immediately, I heard the familiar Momma Cat hiss coming from the other side. I hurried around the outside of my house to the backyard side of the gate and came upon a big, green, non-thorny bush.

The bush was between my house and the shared fence with a neighbor. I found one kitten playing outside the bush and heard a hiss from inside the bush. I moved closer, pulling back some of the bush to reveal Momma Cat and a second kitten inside. Momma Cat hissed louder, and I let the bush go. I wondered, "I only see two kittens. Where are the other three? The bush was big and thick—did I miss seeing them? Are they still underneath the shed, and Momma Cat hasn't had a chance to move them yet?"

This bush resembled an animal's den with its big empty center and a few entry points. The bush provided more accessible access to the kittens than the garden shed. I hoped this was their new nest because it would simplify rounding up the kittens after trapping Momma Cat on Monday.

As it turned out, Momma Cat didn't move her nest to the non-thorny bush. The nest remained under the garden shed. I discovered that Momma Cat used the non-thorny bush as a training ground for her kittens. On a subsequent day, I spied one of the orange tabbies trotting happily behind Momma Cat, coming from the direction of the non-thorny bush and going towards the garden shed.

There were only a few days until Monday—Trapping Day (T-Day). I ordered a pair of Bite-Proof Kevlar Reinforced Leather gloves. They would be delivered the next day. These gloves helped me feel better prepared to deal with Momma Cat. I felt confident that the kittens were still small enough to manage without the gloves.

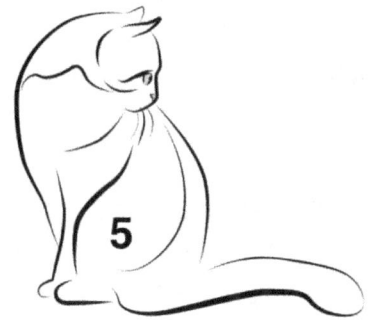

5

A Trapping We Shall Go

Mother's Day arrived, and final preparations were underway to trap Momma Cat (T-Day minus one). I had been moving her food further into the trap for the past few days. Last evening, she went all the way into the trap. Lately, I have been feeding her 3-4 times a day. She had become more assertive—moving closer to my house when she wanted a meal. I suspect the growing kittens' necessity to nurse more often drove her to need more food.

Yesterday, I began feeding her less at each meal so she would be hungrier tomorrow and more likely to go into the trap as planned. I knew following this plan would lead to success; however, I still felt guilty that Momma Cat would be hungry.

I'd make it up to her when she was in my house post-surgery and could eat again. Also, I'd transition the kittens to wet and dry kitten food. Hopefully, they would want to nurse less, and Momma Cat would get a much-needed break.

> **Setting up a cat trap:** Use a stable and sensitive-trigger trap (I used a Tru Catch trap.) Ensure the trap sits flat on a stable surface and securely latch the back of the trap. Ideally, the back of the trap will be up against a wall or other barrier. *{References: Websites: 7a}*

Tomorrow's plan is to trap Momma Cat, round up the kittens, and have the kittens in the house, away from my family's cats. The following day, Momma Cat would rejoin the kittens after her spay surgery. I believe Momma Cat was only nursing the kittens and hadn't taken them to solid food yet. If the kittens didn't immediately transition to the food I would give them, I felt relieved that Momma Cat would still be there. I didn't want to have to give the kittens formula unless necessary. Luckily, Momma Cat could nurse them post-spay surgery. Sage indicated this would provide a nice transitional period for Momma Cat and the kittens, as the kittens would be moving to solid food.

Can mother cats continue nursing after being spayed? Yes. The typical recovery time for cats after spay surgery is 12-24 hours. After recovering, they can resume nursing their kittens. *{References: Websites: 3c}*

Caring for Momma Cat and the kittens after they were inside my house required Momma Cat and me to be a team. I would provide Momma Cat and the kittens with food, water, and clean litter, and she would take care of the kittens' other needs. When the kittens became independent eaters(weaned), I would release Momma Cat to my backyard. I needed time to socialize the kittens, too, and didn't want Momma Cat, a feral cat, to continue teaching the kittens feral ways.

Sage offered me the use of a feral cat den that would allow Momma Cat to stay with the kittens safely.

What is a feral cat den? A feral cat den is like a cube box made of a strong material (polyethylene, for example) with a vertical sliding panel on the front, where the cat initially enters the cat den, perhaps from a cat trap. A circular panel "port door" covers an opening on one side. Use the den to bring the feral cat inside. The den keeps people from getting hurt by aggressive cats and helps keep the feral cats safe. The feral cat den, with the feral cat inside, is typically placed inside a contained space, such as a cage. Open the "port door" to give the cat access to the rest of the cage (litter, food, water, and nursing kittens.) Close the "port door" when the feral cat is in the den and you need to change food, water, and litter in the cage. *{References: Websites: 3d}*

The fact it was Mother's Day and my daughter was away probably contributed to my stronger maternal feelings toward the kittens that day. I started seriously considering what it would be like to foster them. How much time, energy, and possibly money was needed to foster five kittens? How would my husband feel about this? As I considered the answers to these questions, I leaned more heavily toward fostering the kittens. I'd have a test run with them in my house for several days before signing up to officially foster them. This test run would help me to see how I felt about the situation beforehand.

Another consideration when bringing the kittens into the house was whether they were "potty trained" already. How fast kittens take to a litter box varies. Typically, by the age of five weeks, the kittens are used to digging and covering their waste in the dirt, making it easy to transition to a litter box. Just in case, I was planning to use potty pads under the litter box, as Sage had suggested. She also commented that anything that can serve as a low litter box, like the cardboard trays the cat food cans come in, can work well.

I felt concerned that Momma Cat would pull a fast one and move the kittens out of my yard that night. I had a hunch that Momma Cat was within days of moving the kittens again. Trapping Momma Cat tomorrow and rounding up the kittens seemed like good timing.

I asked Sage, "Do the mother cats typically wait until their kittens are a bit older to move them to a community colony?" Sage shared that Momma Cat most likely split off from a nearby group to raise her kittens. The tom cats can be a threat to them. When mother cats go into heat[1], they sometimes leave the kittens for long periods.

I was saddened to hear this. In this way, nature had put even more stress on the mother cats. However, Sage said something else that reassured me that Momma Cat would stay nearby. Sage commented that mother cats tend to raise their kittens

---

1. The reproductive time when a female cat is open to mating. {References: Websites: 1i}

near food sources. As long as I remained a stable food source for Momma Cat, she would have a good reason to keep the kittens in my backyard.

That night, after setting down Momma Cat's food and water, I was on my way towards the back door of my house when she appeared about five feet in front of me, meowing. It wasn't an angry meow, and she seemed to be trying to communicate. I talked to her soothingly, knowing that neither of us could understand the other's language, but at least we were trying.

Then, she turned and ran out of my yard. What had she been trying to say to me? Was she tired and wanted me to help her with the kittens? I believe that was the case. Momma Cat knew I was a regular food source for her, and I hoped that would help get us through the next day. I had been making deposits in my relationship bank account with Momma Cat. Were they enough?

Sage and I discussed whether she would help me trap Momma Cat the next day. We decided against it because Momma Cat might get suspicious and avoid going near the trap if she saw Sage, a stranger to her. I would trap Momma Cat on my own. That Momma Cat was pretty smart, and I needed to stay one step ahead of her. I felt ready to trap her because I had practiced using the trap several times in my garage before setting it up in the backyard.

Time was of the essence to move on this. I wanted the kittens to become socialized to increase their chances for a better life.

I knew the socialization window was closing, and the kittens would eventually become community cats if I didn't do this.

How long is the socialization window for kittens? Generally, 2-8 weeks. After eight weeks (two months), it becomes more challenging to socialize kittens who haven't been around humans. With time and patience, kittens can still be socialized between 2-4 months of age. However, it's much more difficult after the kittens are four months or older. *{References: Websites: 3a}*

Tomorrow, I'd be trapping a cat for the first time. After being captured, I hoped Momma Cat wouldn't become aggressive in the trap, making the situation harder. Sage instructed me to withhold breakfast so Momma Cat would be hungry when I gave her a light lunch in the trap, hopefully catching her then. Each morning recently, Momma Cat had been waiting in the yard for me, and I feared she'd leave the yard to find other food if I didn't give her enough.

At this point, I wanted to trap Momma Cat as soon as possible. I remember Sage mentioning how important it was to reduce Momma Cat's food for a meal or two to build up some hunger and ensure trapping success. I felt guilty about not giving Momma Cat food, but I knew I was new at trapping cats and needed to trust the process.

I reassured myself that this was all for "the cat cause" and that I could do this. Sage reiterated that I was helping Momma Cat and the kittens to have a better future. Since Sage had a lot of experience with this, and she had faith in me, I decided to have faith in myself. My mantra became, "I got this."

The big day, T—day, had arrived. My two main goals were to trap Momma Cat and round up her kittens. Easier said than done. I thought Momma Cat would sense the stress radiating from my body and run off, dashing my hopes that day. I did some meditative breathing before heading outside to attempt the first goal. It was nerve-wracking.

I set up the trap and included some of her usual chicken food inside. After that, she stayed about seven feet away from the trap. I thought, "Oh, no. She's suspicious. I'll give her another 15 minutes and then put some tuna cat food through the back to see if that helps. I think she's pretty hungry, though." It probably didn't help that the trip plate in the trap was a bit of a hump. She wasn't used to that. This hump differed from previous days when she went into the trap, and the food bowl was on flat ground.

I kept my distance from Momma Cat and backed away from the trap, keeping my eyes on her. After a short while, she surprised me by casually walking into the trap and going to the food. I felt euphoric and a bit giddy as I watched the trap door close like it was meant to do. I couldn't believe my eyes—I had just caught Momma Cat! I shared the excellent news with Sage. She gave me a round of congratulations. Whew—I achieved goal one of two for the day. How exciting!

As instructed, I covered the trap with a towel to help keep Momma Cat calm. Then, I moved the trap into the garage—a safe and quiet space. Knowing Momma Cat was hungry, I put some canned salmon kitten food on a big spoon and offered it to her through the trap wire. She devoured the salmon! Keeping in mind she had spay surgery scheduled the next morning, I only gave her a little more. I wanted to give her some food as a bit of a "peace offering" after trapping her. It surprised me how calm Momma Cat was in the trap. She didn't fight being in the trap and seemed like a mellow feral cat to me, just going along with things.

I still needed to retrieve the kittens from underneath the garden shed before nightfall.

Now, on to goal number two - rounding up those kittens!

The Great Kitten Roundup

I walked out to the garden shed to assess the kitten situation. When I looked behind the shed, I saw two kittens playing. Unfortunately, they immediately dove underneath the shed when they saw me. I updated Sage on the situation, and she indicated that we might need to use a trap with the kittens as we did with Momma Cat. If my initial plan to round up the kittens failed, we would trap them.

Only two more hours of daylight remained, causing my anxiety to grow. I still didn't know the kittens' situation under the shed. However, if everything went according to plan, my husband and I would round up the five kittens, place them into a tall plastic bin, and carry them into the house. I had already prepared an area in the house for Momma Cat and the kittens, separate from our three cats. It consisted of a long hallway with a bathroom, office, and guest bedroom connected to it. I planned to borrow a multi-level cage from Sage after settling the kittens into my house.

I looked underneath the shed with a flashlight. I saw two kittens from the original five. There wasn't much visibility due to the narrow space between the dirt and wood platform under the shed. The other kittens could have been hiding in the squirrel tunnels or out of range from the flashlight's beam. My husband and I planned to empty and then move the small shed to gain access to the squirrel tunnels underneath. I hadn't seen the squirrel tunnels before and had no idea how deep they were or where they went. Did they possibly run into the neighbor's yard behind the shed? I hoped not. That would add another level of complexity to an already complicated project.

My husband and I emptied the shed and moved it off the wood platform where it had been sitting. Those were easy tasks. Next, my husband individually pried a few pieces of wood from the platform and decided he could lift the remainder of the platform. I placed the bin nearby to hold the kittens after we retrieved them. Reliving my old softball days, I readied myself to scoop up the kittens.

When my husband lifted the platform, five kittens scurried about in a frenzy. I quickly grabbed one with each hand and placed them into the bin. After I turned back around, I noticed the other three kittens had already dove into the squirrel tunnels. Those kittens were pretty clever. They hadn't been around humans and were doing their best "survival mode" strategy.

That's when the "fun" began for my husband. Those three kittens burrowed themselves further, headfirst, each into a different tunnel. Luckily, the tunnels ran horizontally, so my husband could place one shovel to support the top of the tunnel while using a second shovel to remove the dirt. He had to dig carefully so as not to cause harm to the kitten and avoid causing a dirt cave-in, which would cut off the kitten's oxygen supply.

When I could access about 1/2 of the kitten from the backside, I gently pulled it out with two hands and placed it into the bin. My husband and I continued this process with the next one, and as we continued with the third kitten, unfortunately, there was a dirt cave-in. My stress level rose as my husband and I dug through the dirt quickly to pull out the last kitten. We successfully achieved our goal to "leave no kitten behind!" Although quite dirty, thankfully, the kitten was alive, albeit a bit shaken up. I dusted the kitten off before placing it into the bin.

I carried the bin filled with kittens into the house and placed it into the guest bathroom bathtub. Luckily, Sage had forewarned me that the kitten's natural instincts would be to bite and hiss since they're not used to humans. When I put my hand in to pet the fluffy gray tabby, it stomped down on all four paws simultaneously and did a spitting hiss. It was more cute than frightening to me. I'm sure that's not the effect the kitten hoped to have. It reminded me of a poster that I have of a kitten looking into a mirror and seeing a lion as its reflection. The caption is, "What matters most is how you see yourself." That fluffy gray tabby probably roared in its mind.

I left the stomping kitten in the bin to be the last kitten I cleaned up, to give it a chance to warm up to me by watching my interactions with the other kittens. One by one, I picked up a kitten, wiped the dirt off using a paper towel and a pet wipe (similar to a baby wipe), and wrapped the kitten in a towel, gently drying it off. The kittens seemed to like this last part a lot. Maybe it felt like a massage to them. At this point, all five kittens were squeaky clean and looked healthy. I set them in a clean bin.

Cleaned up kittens in bin

When my husband checked on the kittens and me, I expressed my appreciation: "Thanks for helping me round up the kittens. It was truly a herculean effort on your part—emptying the shed, moving it, pulling up the wood platform underneath, and digging three out of five kittens from squirrel tunnels without losing anyone. What a challenging and dirty job!"

I then followed up with Sage to let her know what had happened. She thought it was an incredible effort. Now, on to feeding the kittens.

I put wet kitten food on two small plates and placed them into the bathtub. Then, I put the kittens around the plates to try the food. Only one of the five kittens ate the wet food, so I drove to a nearby pet store to get some kitten formula to try on them. What a busy evening! I didn't mind, though. I felt relieved that I'd successfully trapped Momma Cat and all five kittens had been safely extracted from underneath the shed. Whew—what a day and an incredible experience!

When I returned home from the pet store, the kittens made my job easier by lapping up the kitten formula in the shallow bowls. Then, I put some fresh, canned kitten food down to try on them again. Imagine my surprise to see all of them eat the canned food on the dishes. It looked like they were ready for food, after all. What a relief!

> 🐾 **Transitioning kittens to wet food**: When moving kittens to wet food for the first time, put a small amount of wet food on a spoon to interest them.
> {References: Websites: 4c}

After focusing so much on Momma Cat and the kittens, I forgot about dinner for my family that night. I checked in on the kittens one more time before I made dinner. They were so cute! When I looked in the bin, three were standing and moving about, and two were lying down, trying to sleep. After dinner, I set up the multi-level cage in the hallway and transferred the kittens into it. Being curious, as cats are prone to be, they started exploring.

I finally had the opportunity to sit down, catch my breath, and rest after a hectic day. I took in the scene with the five beautiful kittens and sent pictures of them to Christina, who responded, "Omg, they're so cute!" I agreed with her. Three kittens were short hairs: the two striped orange tabbies and one striped gray tabby. The two others were long hairs: the black and white tuxedo and fluffy gray tabby, the spirited one who had stomped, hissed, and spit earlier. Christina sent pictures of the kittens to her friends, and they thought they were adorable and, of course, all wanted one.

A natural reaction to seeing kittens is to want one and not think further about whether one has the time, resources, and patience to care for them for the next 15+ years. To a friend,

I said, "A mandatory 'waiting period' is probably necessary because kittens have this effect on us humans."

Although I felt tired that night, I still needed to focus on plans for the next day. My thoughts centered on Momma Cat's spay surgery tomorrow.

I was more than ready for a good night's sleep!

The Assumption Didn't Go Out the Window

The next morning, Momma Cat had her spay surgery, vaccinations, and microchip placement all done. The spay surgery would help reduce the burgeoning feral cat population.

Later that afternoon, I would bring Momma Cat back to my house, where she would remain with her kittens until she recovered from her surgery and the kittens were weaned. Then, I'd release Momma Cat into my backyard. At least, that was the current plan.

What is microchipping for cats? *Microchipping is most often used to reunite lost cats with their caretakers. A small electronic device about the size of a grain of rice, the microchip, is inserted with a needle under the skin between the cat's shoulder blades. The microchip contains a unique number read by a scanner. This number maps to a cat's caretaker's contact information, such as name and phone number. {References: Books: 2, pg.176}*

That day, a long-haired gray cat walked through my backyard and later onto my front porch, probably searching for Momma Cat. One week earlier, I had seen him in my backyard, walking next to Momma Cat in a friendly way. Due to his similar coloring, I guessed he was the father cat to at least two of the kittens.

Can there be more than one father cat per litter of kittens? Yes. Having multiple father cats per litter, known as superfecundation, can happen when a queen mates with different toms during one heat cycle. *{References: Websites: 1j}*

While Momma Cat was away that day, I took the opportunity and thought about fostering the kittens. I decided to foster them for the next 2-3 weeks until they were old enough to be vaccinated, neutered, and all the other requirements to make them adoptable. I wanted to support them in having better lives off the streets and, in so doing, reduce the feral cat population.

I assumed Momma Cat to be feral and, therefore, couldn't be adopted out by animal welfare organizations. Even though feral, I got the sense that, with time and patience, she could be a backyard cat and discourage the squirrels from eating fruit off of my trees. Hopefully, by feeding her, she would stay in my backyard. I shared this possibility with a neighbor, who liked it because Momma Cat could also chase the squirrels from his backyard.

I brought Momma Cat home from her appointment that afternoon and placed the carrier in the bathroom next to the hallway containing the kittens' cage. I closed the door and let Momma Cat roam in the bathroom, giving her space. She surprised me when she quickly jumped onto the bathroom counter and tried to jump through the closed bathroom window. I wasn't ready to release her to the outside since she had just had surgery that day. I needed to keep her inside that night and at least the next day to ensure she healed properly and monitor to see that the kittens were regularly eating without her—weaned.

Momma Cat luckily didn't get hurt. Still disoriented from her surgery, she may have panicked when I let her out of the carrier.

I quickly picked her up and put her back into the carrier, leaving her in the bathroom as I closed the door behind me.

Back in the hallway, I placed two plates of wet food a short distance from the cage. Then I opened the cage, and the kittens pushed past me as if in a race, running towards the wet food. While they were distracted with eating, I grabbed the carrier containing Momma Cat from the bathroom and put it in front of the cage. I opened the carrier so a path for Momma Cat would lead directly into the feral pod. Momma Cat walked into the feral pod and lay down. I closed the cage doors.

Shortly after, the kittens finished eating and walked over to the cage, curiously looking at Momma Cat. I opened the cage doors, and the kittens walked inside. Then, I closed the cage doors. The kittens and Momma Cat reunion wasn't quite what I expected. The kittens seemed wary of Momma Cat and hissed at her. I wondered if Momma Cat had the "vet" smell on her. My cats often hissed at whichever one of them had returned from the vet.

When cats return from the vet, why do nearby cats hiss? Cats' sense of smell is about 14 times stronger than humans. Unknown or strange smells in a cat's environment can cause it to become defensive. After multiple exposures to a smell, cats can become normalized to the smell. *{References: Books: 2, pg. 41}*

All was not lost with this cat family—they worked it out quickly. Momma Cat walked out of the pod and into the central part of the cage. All five kittens approached her and began nursing. Seeing them together now in a warm, safe space was beautiful. That's what I knew. Hopefully, soon, they would feel it was a safe space as they built trust with me.

After a bit, I opened a cage door and watched from a distance to see what Momma Cat would do. She immediately left the cage and went to the kitten food area to eat the leftovers. The effects of the surgery drugs had mainly worn off, and she was hungry, so I gave her a little more food.

I only used the feral pod that first night. Momma Cat didn't act aggressively toward me—what a relief! I felt comfortable not using the pod for the next few days; it was a trial period. If Momma Cat continued not to be aggressive toward humans, I might be able to leave her in the house longer.

I was still considering releasing Momma Cat into the backyard soon. She acted antsy in the cage, trying to roam. The kittens were in the weaning process since they had taken to kitten food so well. Also, I thought it might be easier to socialize the kittens more if Momma Cat wasn't around since she was feral and might interfere. Sage pointed out the kittens' curiosity and said that this was a good age to socialize them.

I decided to release Momma Cat into my backyard that weekend. I felt sad because Momma Cat was such a beautiful and sweet cat, aside from hissing now and then. I wanted her to be an indoor cat, so her life could be better and, most likely, longer. Still, a feral cat is a feral cat—not adoptable.

Momma Cat surprised me a few days later by jumping up on the bathroom counter. I wondered if she would try to go out the window again. I decided this was the right time to let her out to the backyard. The kittens had taken wholeheartedly to the kitten food and didn't need to rely on Momma Cat to nurse them anymore. Momma Cat appeared to have healed well from her surgery, easily jumping high up onto shelves and then back down again.

I opened the bathroom window and coaxed her to go outside. She didn't budge. Instead, she backed away from the window and jumped down on the bathroom floor. One kitten walked over to her and started nursing. Then, the other four ran over. Momma Cat lay down and seemed content because she purred loudly as she nursed her kittens.

What causes cats to purr when they nurse their kittens? 1. It's a way to calm the kittens, letting them know they're safe (it's necessary for newborn kittens since they are born deaf and blind); 2. It's a way to bond with their kittens. *{References: Websites: 1k}*

I wondered if Momma Cat's body naturally reacted to the nursing. If given the choice, would she be done nursing and go outside instead? She didn't act like she wanted to go outside today. I'll see if tomorrow or the day after is different. I had no Plan B yet to release her into the backyard. I had only one plan at that point—out the bathroom window. I didn't want to force it on her. I wasn't sure this was what I wanted to do, either. I liked having Momma Cat around. Also, I suspected the kittens wanted her around. They still wanted to nurse even though they loved the wet and dry kitten food.

After I finished fostering them, I needed to figure out where to take the kittens to be adopted out. My friend, Nadine, knew someone who had previously fostered kittens for the Humane Society. I wanted to see if the Humane Society could take the kittens in a few weeks, and I wanted to understand the process of getting them ready for adoption. Over the years, my family had adopted four kittens from the Humane Society, and I felt a connection with that organization. I knew the other local animal welfare organizations that adopted out kittens were struggling with capacity issues. I hoped the Humane Society might be different and have room for these kittens.

Unfortunately, Nadine's Humane Society contact no longer fostered kittens. Next, Nadine spoke with her son, Ray, who had fostered kittens and worked in a veterinary setting for over a year. He offered to talk with me by phone and give me tips. I jumped at the offer and called him.

I brought Ray up to speed on the situation. I explained my goal was to release Momma Cat into the backyard that weekend. I was informally fostering the kittens for now since so many local cat organizations were experiencing an overwhelming number of kittens that year. I mentioned I could officially sign up to foster the kittens through one of the local organizations. I wanted to find one that wasn't overwhelmed with kittens.

He suggested keeping the kittens and Momma Cat together until they were fully weaned—typically between six and eight weeks. I could get the kittens to six weeks this weekend with Momma Cat. Then, she needed to go back outside. The kittens ate wet and dry food over the past two days and were using the litter box. Since Momma Cat was feral, I needed to get her back outside.

Then Ray planted an idea with me that if Momma Cat was people-friendly, she could get adopted. She might not be feral after all. Hmm, that fits more with what I have been seeing lately. Momma Cat seemed to be friendly overall. I felt like she and I were building a relationship.

Lately, she only hissed at me when surprised, for example, when I opened the slider door to the hallway. I can only imagine she didn't know what to expect, so she hissed as a warning to whatever was opening that door. I also wondered if she was a bit stressed and feeling protective because she was still nursing the kittens. Maybe she would be more relaxed when no longer nursing them.

Ray also emphasized not to give the kittens to a place where they might be adopted out before they were weaned. He explained that since the kittens were about 5-6 weeks old, Momma Cat would start to walk away or move them off when they tried to nurse. This was part of the weaning process. I remarked that they were already weaned and continuing to nurse because she was still around and allowed it at times.

> **Weaning kittens:** Typically, the weaning process starts at about five weeks of age. Patience is important during this time to let weaning happen on the kittens' timeframe. Starting kittens with high-quality wet kitten food is good for their health. *{References: Websites: 4c}*

He stressed the importance of keeping the kittens away from my family's cats until the kittens had been vaccinated and my cats' shots were all up to date. The kittens' immune systems weren't mature enough yet. One consideration was that the kittens shouldn't even touch the floor my cats touched. Another consideration is that humans and other pets in the household can bring in debris and infectious material from outside. I decided that until the kittens were vaccinated, I would put on socks I only wore in the kittens' area (a clean pair each day) and a long shirt over my other shirt to avoid contaminating the kittens' environment.

Initially, keep other household animals away from kittens: Kittens may have contagious diseases, larger animals may hurt the kittens, and it can be stressful for all animals. *{References: Websites: 1l}*

Ray recommended a feral kitten video from the "Kitten Lady" website to help me socialize the kittens.

Socializing feral kittens: "From Wild to Mild" video. *{References: Websites: 4d}*

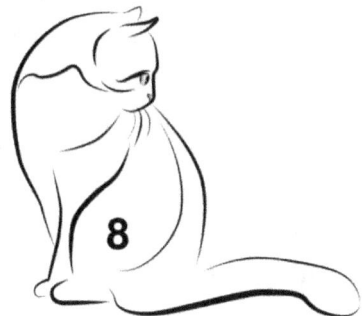

8

Attached? Not Me!

T he next day, I texted Christina, "I can't afford to get attached to the kittens. They are going to other homes eventually. I'll probably still get attached to them." Only time will tell.

My husband and I set up 24/7 viewing of the kittens in their hallway via the cat cam so Christina could enjoy watching them play. Unfortunately, this served as an effective form of advertisement for the kittens and caused Christina to become attached to them. My good intentions backfired.

Christina began negotiating to take one of the kittens. She had fine-tuned her negotiation skills during her teen years. My resolve to not keep a kitten weakened as Christina played to my sentimental side, reminding me that the kittens were raised in our backyard, and that's special.

She asked me questions about the softness of the kittens' fur. She loved petting cats with soft fur. The two long-haired kittens—gray tabby and tuxedo—were so fluffy and soft, with the litter's softest fur. The other three were somewhat soft, too.

The long-haired gray kitten looked like he belonged on the cover of "Kitten Vogue" magazine because he was so photogenic. When his eyes capture you in their gaze, you can't help wanting to pet and play with him. That explained why I seemed to take a disproportionate amount of pictures of that one.

"Vogue" kitten in book box

I told Christina the kittens wouldn't stay in this ultra-cute state forever. That's why it's important to consider their temperament. Also, how humans socialize them can make a big difference. This goes back to the old "Nature vs. Nurture" discussion. I believe it's important to consider both Nature (what they're born with—temperament, physical characteristics) and Nurture (environmental effects on them that affect their personalities.)

The long-haired gray one was the bravest and fastest of the litter. He was the first to climb to the top of the multi-level cage. My heart skipped a beat when I saw him up there the first time. Then, one of the orange tabbies "copy-catted" him. Then, the second orange tabby followed that one. I would take them off the top of the cage, set them down on the floor, and within a minute, they'd be at the top again. I finally sat down for a while and watched the kittens climbing around on the cage. I determined they could safely climb up and down on their own.

 Kitten-proof for tall objects: Move tall objects that kittens may fall off of to another room. *{References: Books: 1, pgs.72-73}*

The kittens were cuddly and cute. All five were quite curious, and they kept me busy. As they grew, so did their capabilities. I spent quite a bit of time herding those kittens out of trouble. To help with this, I borrowed a cat scratcher tower since the kittens needed something to scratch instead of my books in the hallway.

Recently, I have been checking into available animal welfare organizations that might be able to adopt the kittens. I chose one and officially registered as a foster for the kittens. I wanted to be a part of the solution. I didn't want five more cats eventually out there reproducing exponentially. Also, I wanted them to have a chance at a better life.

This was really happening. I was officially fostering five kittens! The next step was to set up an intake appointment for the kittens, at which time their photos would be taken, their weights recorded, and their initial dewormer treatment would be done.

While fostering them, I would be provided with flea medicines, food, and litter. They would also receive their first vaccines. This was helpful since the cat care for those five kittens was already adding up. I was fully committed and wanted to give them the best start in their lives.

My commitment would be approximately two weeks at this point. Before spay/neuter surgery, the kittens must weigh about two pounds, be at least eight weeks old, and be healthy. Then, my fostering would officially end, and I'd turn them over to be prepared for adoption.

Now, what to do with Momma Cat? I still doubted her being a feral cat, especially after my phone call with Ray. When I next texted Sage, I said, "I'm working on my relationship with Momma Cat and building trust with her. I spoon-fed her for a bit today. She's a sweet girl and a pretty calm feral. Since she is feral, I'm being cautious, too." Sage was surprised Momma Cat had eaten off of a spoon and thought she probably wasn't feral after all.

I was conflicted. I still considered releasing Momma Cat into my backyard that weekend. I didn't know if she could become an indoor cat. My husband and I figured out another way to get her to the backyard using the child safety gates we still had around. However, Ray and Sage separately mentioned that Momma Cat was possibly a shy community cat, which caused me to pause in taking action on this.

Sage also commented that most feral cats will run when given the chance. The day before, Momma Cat resisted going outside when I gave her the chance.

Maybe she was a young cat who had grown up outside, born to a community cat, and was not used to being inside. More socialization would likely increase her trust in humans. She seemed more shy than actually feral, but feral is a continuum.

After more consideration, I finally concluded that Momma Cat was not feral. What convinced me was Momma Cat's behavior towards me. Momma Cat walked up to me, allowing me to pet her, and hissed less. I started picking her up off the floor about one foot and carrying her to her food every so often to get her used to being picked up. Also, she purred so loudly that you could hear her from across the room.

Since I would be fostering the kittens for at least two more weeks, I would keep Momma Cat indoors and continue socializing her during that time so she could eventually be adopted. Her future adopters would need to have experience with cats and give her the necessary love and patience for her situation.

I would have adopted her in a heartbeat if there weren't three cats in our household. I was becoming attached to Momma Cat.

I took a moment to reflect on how far I had come with Momma Cat and the kittens. Dealing with what I thought was a feral cat and her five kittens had been a lot of work and stress, even though they were all so adorable. This is not something I ever planned, but since Momma Cat chose my backyard, I wanted to help with the situation. Momma Cat was talking to me in a nicer meow tone now, with less hissing, and seemed to trust me with her kittens, too.

Momma Cat probably appreciated me playing with her kittens. This gave her a break since they were still nursing. Momma Cat acted more like she was ready to be done nursing. Sometimes, when a kitten ran up to her and started nursing while she was standing, Momma Cat quickly walked away or jumped onto a bookcase too high for the kittens to reach.

I marveled at how good Momma Cat was with her kittens. I heard her set boundaries with a particular meow tone when the kittens pushed her too much, nursing being one example. Another time, she let out a high-pitched meow when they played in the litter box while she was using it. To show a-ffection to her kittens, she rubbed against them. I couldn't imagine dealing with five at one time. Sage pointed out that by nature, mother cats care for their kittens' by nursing and grooming. I thought about how humans can try and do their best with kittens when a mother cat can't care for them. However, if the mother cat is around, it's usually, "Mother cat knows best!"

My biggest challenge at that point wasn't Momma Cat and the kittens; it was Christina. She wanted to take a kitten back to college, and I was concerned that she wouldn't have enough time for it. Fortunately, there was still time for more discussions about that and other kitten care concerns. I had at least two weeks left to foster five kittens.

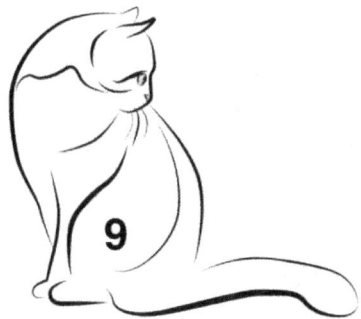

9

Fostering—Another Word for Love

Fostering is another word for love. This refers to the love I got from the kittens and the love I gave to them. The more time I spent with them, the more comfortable we all became with each other.

Fostering five kittens was fulfilling and exhausting. I imagine fostering just one or two kittens at their age—six weeks—would be easier. Either way, I'd still be caring for our three cats simultaneously, with cats and kittens in two different spaces.

That night, I moved the cat cam to a better location for Christina to see the kittens. She loved watching them. Christina felt sad that she had missed experiencing the kittens when they were indoors by one week. At least she got to pet them a little when they were outside before she left for her summer program.

When I came out the next morning, I was disappointed that Momma Cat had chewed through the cat cam cable. Her large teeth marks were all over it. After this, my husband moved the cat cam and cable above the office door onto hooks so Momma Cat couldn't reach them.

That was a big day for the kittens. All five would get their vaccinations, and everything else needed for me to officially foster them. When the time came to head over, they didn't make it easy for me to put them into the carrier. These kittens had become bigger and faster. My valid excuse for being late to their appointment was kitten herding problems.

When I dropped them off, a worker took each kitten to weigh, take a photo, and do the rest of what was needed to create an information sheet to identify the kitten. A couple standing nearby saw the kittens and commented on how cute they were. They appreciated them so much that I thought they would try to adopt them right there and then! Of course, this wouldn't have been possible. However, I understand how they felt because the kittens were quite cute.

Everything went smoothly at the kittens' appointment. When I picked them up that afternoon, I also picked up the supplies—food, litter, and bowls. Their adoption intake appointment was in two weeks.

Having the kittens in the house made it much easier to notice their growth. It seemed like they had gotten bigger overnight. They still demanded to be nursed. However, I noticed Momma Cat stopped nursing them sooner than the previous week. I imagined her ready to be done with nursing.

However, the kittens had another idea, and there were five of them! When the kittens returned from their appointment, they ran over and piled on top of Momma Cat to nurse. It looked as if the kittens tackled Momma Cat in a football game.

Kittens tackled Momma Cat

My official foster time had begun! The estimated plan was that the kittens would be ready for adoption in two weeks. Every day, I needed to record information on each kitten on a sheet, including their weight, the type of food eaten, toileting habits, activity level, and any noted health issues. I viewed this fostering work as a "labor of love."

One problem I encountered that day was with the new collars containing the kittens' ID numbers. One of the orange tabby kittens managed to get its paw stuck in the collar. I decided to take all of the collars off. That was fine for three of them since I could tell them apart by their coloring. However, that theory didn't work well with the two orange tabbies. They were nearly identical-looking and were females.

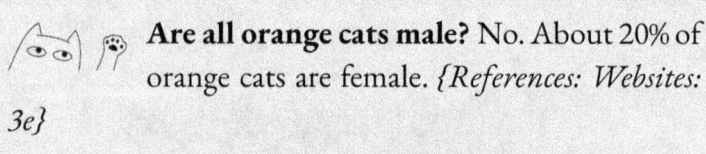

Are all orange cats male? No. About 20% of orange cats are female. *{References: Websites: 3e}*

I placed the break-away collar I had been given on one of the orange tabbies. I watched it for a bit. This cat was so active that the collar kept coming off. Luckily, I found a differentiator for those two orange tabbies since the collar wasn't working. One orange tabby was heavier than the other, but I didn't want to go by weight as the differentiator since that can fluctuate based on health, too. I discovered that one orange tabby had a light circle on each side near her tail. That became the differentiator I needed.

How do you tell a cat's breed from its markings? Alley Cat Allies—Cat Identification Guide covers seven topics—coat length, coat color, coat patterns, markings, feature colors, unique identifiers, and determining sex. *{References: Websites: 3e}*

I developed routines with Momma Cat and the kittens to make my fostering easier. One such routine helped reduce Momma Cat's hissing when I entered the hallway. Before I opened the hallway door, I shuffled papers around to make some noise on my side to signal Momma Cat and the kittens that someone would be opening the door. This helped to prevent them from becoming startled, especially Momma Cat.

Because the kittens were getting faster and faster, it became necessary to leave a wood barrier in place when opening the hallway door. They still darted past me several times when I wasn't quick enough to replace the barrier after entering the hallway.

As Momma Cat became more restless, I allowed her and the kittens to roam into the bathroom while preparing to feed them and clean their litter box. This allowed them to stretch their legs more. I ensured that Momma Cat and the kittens were back in the hallway and that the bathroom door was closed before leaving. I made a habit of counting heads before I left that hallway area.

I established a protocol to have two pairs of socks for cat care. I wore one pair in Momma Cat and the kittens' area and the other in the area where our three cats resided. I took care of Momma Cat and the kittens first and then went into the other cat area. Also, I had a long T-shirt I threw over my top when I went into the kitten area. This was important because the kittens' immune systems weren't yet mature. Also, it was important to remember to wash my hands before going between cat areas.

The morning feeding needed to happen by 9 a.m.—apparently due to their internal feeding clock. If not fed by then, Momma Cat and the kittens would meow loudly. I quickly weighed each kitten, and after all five were done, I fed them and Momma Cat their breakfast.

To keep a kitten contained when weighing it: Place a bowl on the scale (Make a note of the bowl's weight to subtract from the total weight later to obtain the kitten's weight.) Put the kitten in the bowl, and make a circle with your hands, with the kitten in the middle, without touching it. *{Becky's tip}*

Because the kittens were so active, it was essential to have plenty of water available to them—two bowls. Momma Cat was still nursing and drinking more water than the average cat. I kept her water bowl up high inside the cage so she'd have easy access.

> **Keep cats hydrated.** Water is critical to a cat's health, and it's important to provide them with a separate water source, even if they're eating wet cat food. Keep their water source away from litter boxes, or the cats may avoid drinking the water. Provide multiple sources of water for cats around the home. *{References: Books: 1, pgs.32-33}*

Since the kittens were in their growing phase and Momma Cat was nursing, I left dry food out all day, refilling twice a day, without worrying about them gaining too much weight. I couldn't do this with our three grown cats because I needed to control how often they ate dry food. If not, their vet would lecture me at their next appointment weigh-in.

> **Dry food is - dry:** Cats exclusively on dry food diets, especially male cats, run a higher risk of urinary problems. Providing wet cat food is important because some cats won't drink enough water on their own. *{References: Books: 2, pg.135}*

Momma Cat showed her hunger level based on her movement towards the wet food. If she wasn't as hungry, she stayed back and let the kittens eat first. If she was hungry, she dove in, displacing kittens in the way. I started giving Momma Cat a separate plate of food, encouraging the kittens to spread out and mostly go to a second plate. I used to begin with three plates but then noticed food got wasted that way. I went to more of a "wait and see" on whether to give a third small can of food. With the small cans, it was easier to avoid wasting uneaten food. I've noticed that my cats generally don't like cold food, so I didn't want to refrigerate the uneaten food. These were growing kittens, so I knew I'd be able to switch to large cans soon.

I broke the food into smaller pieces and avoided putting food in the middle, instead putting it in a circle on the outer part of the plate. If all kittens weren't going to the food, I might need to bring whoever wasn't over to the food. Sometimes, they were just distracted playing and didn't notice the food.

After eating, the kittens often liked to scratch or nap on the cardboard scratchboard that I had put in the hallway. Momma Cat and the kittens could use it instead of trying to scratch the hardwood floor. I wasn't worried about the floor but about keeping their claws healthy.

By this time, I had two litter boxes on the cage floor. I used the pine litter since clumping litter can be unsafe for kittens. I noticed it needed to be changed out more often than clumping litter. I used clumping litter with my adult cats in the other part of the house.

I had backup litter boxes for Momma Cat and the kittens, so every few days, I could swap out the entire box and swap in a clean one. I got into a cleaning rhythm with this and the cage floor, which needed cleaning twice daily. The cat wipes were a big help, although using paper towels with water on them probably was a more cost-effective way to do it.

Why can clumping litter be unsafe for kittens? Kittens may play in the litter, licking it off themselves and swallowing it while grooming, increasing their chance of experiencing intestinal and stomach blockages. *{References: Websites: 1m}*

That evening, Momma Cat nursed the five kittens in front of the slider door, blocking my exit from the hallway. They were too cute! Although I felt tired and wanted to get to bed, there was no way I would break up that sweet family scene. Luckily, I didn't have long to wait. Momma Cat only nursed the kittens for about five minutes at a time now. As the kitten party broke up, I saw my opening to the door and headed off to bed, thoroughly exhausted.

I wasn't the only one who was exhausted. Recently, when I opened the doorway to the hallway, I noticed Momma Cat coming over, standing there, appearing tired and looking longingly over the wood barrier. I think she secretly plotted how to jump over it and past me.

*Momma Cat protective
or contemplating escape?*

As part of the kittens' socialization, I needed to play with them. Playtime with the kittens was the easiest part of caring for them. I left safe toys strewn on the hallway floor. I also put the rolly balls up when no one was actively playing with them so we wouldn't accidentally trip on them at other times. The kittens (and Momma Cat) were so much fun! I especially enjoyed watching them chase the "mice" attached to the end of the string I pulled around on the floor.

My household cats seemed out of sorts with the kittens around. The kittens required more attention for socialization before being adopted, so I had less time to spend with our cats. I'm guessing it upset them that they were getting less attention from me. Just that morning, one of our cats bumped up against the door I was sitting on the other side of, demanding my attention.

Later that night, with my husband out of town, I sat alone with our cats, watching TV in my family room. Suddenly, I heard a loud bang against the family room window. It caused me to jump up off of the couch. Our cat, Leia, sat on the loveseat below that window, looking out at the source of the noise. It was the suspected father of the kittens.

He had apparently thrown himself against the window, maybe to get to Leia. He stared at us from the other side of the window. It was pretty unsettling. I stared back at him, and he looked back at me like he owned the place. A very brazen boy! He might have been on the prowl, looking for Momma Cat.

Suspected father cat looking in

This episode unnerved me. Luckily, I was exhausted from taking care of the nine cats in my care and fell asleep pretty quickly.

In one week, I'd be done fostering the kittens, and they would go to be prepared for adoption. All the kittens were growing well and eating wet food twice daily, along with dry food available throughout the day. They were adorable handfuls!

I hoped to make it to their drop-off appointment with my sanity intact. After I handed off the five kittens, only Momma Cat would be left to adopt out. I hoped she could be fully socialized by me and then adopted out by a local animal organization. If not, I needed to privately adopt her out, ensuring that the person who adopted her knew how to work with her. Usually, I could pet her and pick her up, to a point. I needed to see how she was without the kittens around. My guess was they were getting on her nerves as they got bigger.

However, every time I thought Momma Cat was done nursing, she wasn't. It took just one kitten to start nursing, then she would lie down, and the rest of the kittens ran over and joined in. She didn't nurse for very long each time, but it still surprised me that she continued to do it.

That day, while taking a video of the kittens, I accidentally set the video in time-lapse mode. It was funny watching them chase after each other in that super-fast mode. The kittens were getting so fast that the time-lapse mode seemed like it would soon be the reality.

Also, I captured the kittens climbing inside and outside the cage on video. The kittens easily climbed to the top of the cage. I had considered trimming their claws so they wouldn't scratch me when they jumped on my pant legs. Trimming their claws could cause them to be unable to grab onto the cage, potentially falling to the ground. I didn't trim their claws.

I noticed my husband occasionally having fun with the kittens. His toy of choice - the laser pointer. Those lively kittens loved to chase after that red dot. I dubbed my husband the "kitten whisperer" because he seemed to have control over them when he used the laser pointer. I enjoyed watching them jump onto the wall and scramble after each other as they chased the red dot.

Days later, Christina pushed me again to keep one kitten. She thought the black one with the white paws was the cutest. He became quite the lap cat. He climbed onto my lap when I cleaned a litter box—extremely adorable and made the litter box cleaning more interesting. He also played a lot with one of my favorite kittens, the fluffy gray one. Initially, this gray one seemed to be Christina's favorite kitten to watch from the cat cam. However, now that she was serious about wanting one, she didn't know whether she wanted the fluffy gray or black and white one.

Picking the right cat for yourself: This is a subset of questions to ask yourself when choosing a cat: Do you want a kitten or an adult cat? Do you want a male or female cat? Do you want a particular breed of cat? Do you want an active or more calm cat? *{References: Book: 2, pg.64-65}*

The fluffy gray one seemed the most mature out of the bunch and a good climber. He might be Christina's best choice. Either way, she couldn't go wrong with whichever of those two that she chose. I noticed they played with their other brother and sisters, too, but seemed to hang out the most with each other. I affectionately dubbed those two "The Boys."

I asked Christina some important questions: "How would keeping a kitten work for you? We must consider the setup in our house with our three cats (and possibly Momma Cat) until you can take the kitten. Also, which one would you take? It would be hard to choose."

I had been around so many cats that I thought I was having a "cat fever," causing me not to think realistically about the kitten situation. I considered holding onto one for Christina until she could take it. However, she had to make up her mind soon. There were only six days left until adoption time.

I would miss the kittens. Why are kittens made to be so cute? Although caring for them was a fun and exciting experience, I needed to remember that I hadn't planned for this—they showed up in my backyard. The kittens appeared when my mantra had been, "I need to simplify my life." I felt the universe testing me on this.

Feeling tired the next morning, without thinking, I stuck my head inside the cage as I set down the clean litter box. Usually, I slid the litter box in when Momma Cat was inside. Unfortunately, that morning, my head appeared right in front of Momma Cat and surprised her. She tapped the top of my head with her paw, which I took as a warning. I don't blame her. In retrospect, she probably felt cornered, with nowhere to go. Luckily, her defensive move didn't include her claws.

We needed to work on rebuilding our relationship because I noticed she kept her distance from me the rest of the day. I needed to help her feel safer and trust people more in order to be an indoor cat for someone else someday. We'll see. I worked on opening more rooms to give her space to roam. I think her growing kittens and their demands were causing her to be stir-crazy.

I kitten-proofed my home office so the kittens could wander there while I was working. They loved running into my office when I opened the door, jumping onto the chairs, and then the desk. They often snuck past me before I realized, and I had to corral and remove them from the room before an online meeting began. A few times, the ailurophiles[1] on a meeting call wanted to see a kitten or two when they heard about them, so I obliged and brought kittens into the room.

At that time, my desk reflected the saying from Albert Einstein, a 20th-century theoretical physicist: "If a cluttered desk is a sign of a cluttered mind, of what, then, is an empty desk a sign?" This meant many papers on my desk were waiting to be knocked off, which the kittens did.

---

1. A cat fancier; a lover of cats {References: Websites: 6f)

Even though the kittens were adorable, and I enjoyed fostering them, I was glad most were moving on to their next life adventure in five days. Their energy overwhelmed me! I began taking a mini-nap every afternoon. I didn't plan on this fostering adventure but felt glad to help the cat community.

A few days later, I spoke with Christina about having a workable plan if she wanted to take one of the kittens. She needed to step back and consider the work involved with having a kitten. She agreed to work on a plan. Then she told me that one of her friends wanted a kitten, too. She reminded me that these kittens needed good homes. Christina didn't play fair—pulling on my heartstrings like that.

My husband had already planned to drive a car across the country for Christina to use. Also, he would help Christina move into her apartment then. For a brief moment, we considered him taking the two kittens in the car and then thought better. Traveling for 5-6 days in a car with kittens was a recipe for disaster— probably more so for my husband's sanity. Another thought—Christina could fly back home for a weekend and bring the kittens back with her. That sounded more feasible, and we ditched the driving-in-the-car idea.

As the kittens continued growing, they became more mischievous. One of their favorite tricks was climbing into the bathtub supply bins and pulling things out. When they were smaller, this wasn't a problem. Now that they were bigger, I needed to ensure the lids were firmly on the bins when I left the bathroom. That morning, when I opened the door into the hallway, I saw the green cat litter waste bags stretching into the hallway from the bathtub. I'd check the cat cam recordings later to see which kittens had fun pulling the litter bags out of the bin.

The kitten situation became more complicated as time went on. Christina loved to travel, so she had to figure out how to care for her cat while away. I thought, "I may regret this decision, or it may work out wonderfully. I hope, I hope." I knew there were kittens where Christina lived; however, the kittens from our backyard would have special significance for her. We found them in our backyard, and I fostered them so Christina knew their background. A family connection would always exist and felt like a beautiful cat story.

Soon, the plan finally came together—adopt two kittens, The Boys, and eventually deliver them to Christina and her friend. I had planned to visit Christina during the summer since it was a long time until Thanksgiving. I decided in six weeks, I'd fly across the country with the kittens in a cat carrier under the seat in front of me. The cat travel cost would be $75 for both, and logistics needed to be worked out.

Good news for Momma Cat—she would spend another six weeks with two of her kittens. That delayed me from having to decide her next step. This may be enough time to finish the socialization needed so she can be adopted.

I was set to drop off the five kittens the next day to be readied for adoption, their spay/neuter surgeries being part of this. After that, my big task would be to pick up the two I was adopting. When I dropped the kittens off in the morning, I planned to make sure it was clear which two I planned to adopt.

Knowing this was our last night with all the kittens, my husband took the opportunity to play with them with the laser pointer. The kittens loved chasing it! I wondered if my husband couldn't help but get attached to these cute kittens. I know Christina did. She would have taken all of the kittens if she could have. They were so cute!

Adoption— Bittersweet

On the morning of their spay/neuter surgeries, I gave the kittens a small breakfast. When it was time to drop them off, I mused, "If only I could pick their homes." All were adorable, playful, and sweet kittens. I felt protective and wanted them to be cared for and loved.

When I handed over the kittens, I gave the intake person the foster sheets for the two I planned to adopt that afternoon to avoid hiccups in the process. It was important, especially for Christina and her friend, to ensure I got the kittens they chose. They had watched the kittens on the cat cam and had become attached to them.

While the kittens were being prepared for adoption, Momma Cat walked around my house, meowing sadly. It was painful to hear. Petting her didn't seem to help, either. I felt terrible about taking all five kittens away at once, but it was the best way to deal with this situation. She didn't know that two of them would return that afternoon.

I took this opportunity to clean up the multi-level cage, cat scratch post, and a litter box that Sage had loaned me. Going from Momma Cat and five kittens to Momma Cat and two kittens already sounded more manageable. I looked forward to seeing how the dynamics between Momma Cat and the kittens changed once there were two instead of five.

Reflecting on the three kittens staying behind that day to be adopted out, those two orange tabbies and one gray-striped tabby had been so cute and playful. However, the orange tabbies were the ring leaders of the kittens regarding bad behavior, and the gray-striped tabby followed after them. For example, they created a game of jumping on my pant legs. It took patience, energy, retraining, and a few pairs of scratched-up pants before the kittens stopped that bad habit.

I also reflected on all that had happened. Whew—what an experience! I was so appreciative of all the help Sage had given me with the kittens. This experience had been a team effort, with her coaching me and providing much-needed support.

That afternoon was bittersweet when I picked up the two kittens in their carrier after I officially adopted them. On the one hand, I felt relieved that three would be staying behind that day, and on the other hand, I felt sad because I would miss them, too.

And then there were two—kittens, that is. I returned home later that afternoon with The Boys. Momma Cat's happy reaction to having them back with her was a beautiful sight. She rubbed up against them and licked them. The three of them looked like the sweetest little family together. I dubbed them "The Littles Family" in contrast to my family's larger-sized household cats.

I texted Christina about the situation and said, "We were lucky to have all those kittens in our lives for the time we had them. What a gift! Momma Cat is happy to have some of her kitties back. The three of them are spending afternoon nap time together."

I contacted Sage with a kitten update. I commented that the kittens had been pretty spirited, loving, and playful. Sage declared the kittens to be a lovely success story.

The Boys had settled down a bit now without the other three kittens around. I admit, I was relieved we were down to two kittens; the energy level was noticeably reduced. Also, that afternoon was the first time I heard the fluffy gray kitten purr—how precious!

I shouldn't have been surprised later to see The Boys nursing again. Poor Momma Cat! Would nursing never end? Of course, The Boys were going off to their forever homes in another month or so. That's when Momma Cat would be done with nursing, for sure.

Christina wanted the fluffy gray kitten, and her friend wanted the black and white one. My husband and I temporarily named them "Little Gray" and "Tux" since he had white on his chest like a tuxedo. "Little Climber" probably would have been more appropriate for Christina's kitten because he loved climbing up everything. It didn't take him long to climb up on the bed in the guest bedroom. I put a lot of books from the bookshelves in the hallway on that bed when I needed to kitten-proof the hallway early on. Now, my cluttered piles of books on the bed were no longer safe from that little climber.

The next day, I sent Christina pictures of the new cat setup. It consisted of no cage, one litter box in the bathroom, a new cat tower in the hallway with attached scratching posts, a more permanent setup for food and water, and a less stressed me. One of the pictures was of The Boys stretched out in their new cat bed, a "Welcome Back" gift after their adoption. Those kittens were adorable, asleep or awake!

The Boys catnapping

I took my job of socializing the kittens and Momma Cat very seriously. That was my excuse for my extended periods of petting and playing with them. The importance of taking frequent kitten breaks should not be underestimated, though. I now understand the concept of "support animals" in helping reduce stress. Petting Momma Cat and the kittens and playing with them helped me to relax.

I needed to go out of town for a quick overnight trip, so I did a mini-training for my husband on cat care for Momma Cat and The Boys. Cat care was much easier now that the kittens were bigger and there were only two. It also helped that Momma Cat seemed to trust us humans more. My husband took good care of them. However, he ignored my instruction to hug the kitties good night before he turned their light out at bedtime. He prefers to leave that to me.

One 5.5 oz. can of kitten food twice daily and unlimited dry food worked for The Littles Family. I used a water pitcher twice daily to replenish their water bowls. After rinsing the water bowl out in the morning, I replaced it with a fresh bowl every afternoon.

Taking care of the litter box was a work in progress. I swapped to a taller litter box because as the kittens grew, they knocked the litter out of the shorter box. Twice a day, I scooped out the box, and about twice a week, I completely cleaned out the box. That meant I went through a lot of litter. I bought the 40-pound bag of pine litter to save money. My husband agreed to take on the job of "mover of the litter." My back thanked him!

The week after the adoption, I texted Ray to share my appreciation for his previous wise counsel regarding Momma Cat. I'm so thankful I didn't put her back outside along the way!

The kittens, now nine weeks old, and Momma Cat seemed more relaxed and interacted well with my husband and me. Two aspects probably helped this—there were only two kittens now, and Momma Cat wasn't letting The Boys nurse as much these days. Still, every time I thought Momma Cat had quit nursing, one of The Boys came over to nurse again, with the second joining in soon after. At this point, I suspect the nursing fell more under the category of "comfort nursing." Basically, The Boys nursing out of habit and keeping their connection with Momma Cat.

I allowed the kittens to roam outside their hallway into the living room while supervising them. My husband and I set up the child safety gates—the ones we didn't use when we thought Momma Cat was feral—to create a mini "hallway." This hallway ran from the kitten area, extending in front of the fireplace to the glass door separating the living room from the family room.

The Boys plotting their next move

Momma Cat and The Boys could see our three cats through the glass door and vice versa. Initially, I put towels under the door to fill the gap so The Littles Family and our three cats couldn't spread germs to each other.

Both cat families hanging out

I planned to integrate Momma Cat and The Boys with my cats in the next few weeks so The Littles Family could become comfortable with other animals outside their family. It would also be more interesting for the cats to hang out together. It was easier said than done since ensuring none of my cats hurt The Littles Family and vice versa was important. All cats were up to date with their vaccinations. Since they had been outdoors recently, The Littles Family had also been tested for Feline Leukemia (FeLV) and Feline AIDS (FIV).

What are Feline Leukemia Virus (FeLV) and Feline AIDS (FIV)? Both are incurable diseases specific to cats and suppress a cat's immune system, allowing other illnesses to affect the cats. Depending on the cat's care and circumstances, they may live full lives. There is a standard vaccine available for FeLV. *{References: Websites: 1n, 1o}*

As if things weren't interesting enough with six cats in my house, The Boys' suspected father cat still hung around my yard. He lived up to the phrase "peeping tom" because a few times a week, he would peek in on us at night through the large family room window while we watched TV—a bold guy.

I changed the setup for The Littles Family. Now, they could freely roam the hallway and bathroom. I opened the guest bedroom to let them roam there during the day. Little Gray and Tux, in true kitten fashion, were very curious and got into trouble. After not readily finding them one day, I discovered those sweet kittens, each curled up in a ball, sleeping on the pull-out tray of the desk. It looked to be a good hideaway.

I took The Littles Family back into the hallway and closed the guest bedroom door in the evenings. I couldn't trust the kittens not to get into trouble in the bedroom at night. I kitten-proofed it to a point, but I still needed to finish so I could comfortably let them roam there even while I was asleep.

My husband and I were heading out of town soon, and I needed to share Momma Cat and the kittens' setup with our cat care provider. When anybody other than myself or my husband entered the hallway, Momma Cat moved into the bathroom. When the guest bedroom door was opened, she'd run underneath the bed.

Initially, The Boys might go with her until they get used to the humans. Their rainbow stick toy had worked 100% of the time to get all three of them out of that room, and then I quickly closed the door. Since Momma Cat was more skittish, she might sometimes resist coming out if she didn't know the person. The cat care provider and I agreed that leaving the bedroom door open overnight was okay if that were the case. It wasn't ideal, but if Momma Cat wouldn't come out of the room, then the door needed to remain open for her to get to food, water, and the litter box.

> **Approaching skittish cats:** Cats can take a little bit to warm up to strangers. Ensure the cats have a "safe spot" to retreat to, like under a bed. *{References: Books: 2, pg. 75}*

Sure enough, when we went out of town and the cat care provider came over, Momma Cat and The Boys did their disappearing act under the bed. Momma Cat stayed under the bed, and The Boys initially hid under the bed with her. Tux came out first since now he was the braver of the two. Little Gray then followed his lead after a bit. Opening a can of food would sometimes encourage The Boys to come out faster, but on the cat care provider's initial visit, they weren't making it ea sy.

All the supplies for Momma Cat and the kittens now resided in two bins in the guest bathroom bathtub. Before the cat care provider arrived one morning, the kittens had pulled the green litter bags from the bin to the litter box. Those little rascals! The cat care provider and I laughed at the kittens' hint that the litter box needed cleaning. Apparently, the kittens had a lot of fun while we humans were gone. Also, the kittens unrolled the toilet paper. No more leaving toilet paper out in that bathroom. When I returned, I would work on breaking them of that habit. If I weren't successful, Christina and her friend would get to work on that with The Boys.

Another fun challenge those days was sweeping the bathroom floor after cleaning the litter box. The kittens loved jumping up on the broom and biting the bristles. They seemed to enjoy this game of "kittens vs. the broom." On days I didn't have the time, I would move the kittens into the hallway, close the bathroom door, and sweep unhindered and in peace.

Christina came for a short, last-minute visit to see The Boys. This was the first time she'd seen them inside the house, and I felt it was good for her to interact with them before taking them next month. She would have taken them back then but needed to wait to get into her fall housing.

She enjoyed seeing The Boys and connected well with both kittens. These kittens were getting cuter with time as their personalities continued developing. Also, Christina liked Momma Cat and suggested I keep her. I liked Momma Cat, too, but we already had three cats.

Another change in plans occurred a few days after Christina left, just weeks before I was to take the kittens to Christina and her friend. The friend's circumstances changed, and she could no longer take the kitten, Tux. Christina now considered taking both kittens so they could stay together. We didn't know if this was a possibility where Christina would live. Maybe having the two wouldn't be so bad. They could keep each other company when Christina was out. Things just got more complicated. I remembered the plan was to simplify my life this year. Oh, well, that wasn't happening anytime soon.

I admit I enjoyed having The Littles Family in my life. However, I feared that I had become attached to them. From this cat-fostering experience, I learned that I wanted to avoid a "foster fail" in the future if I volunteered to foster kittens again. I would do this by being clear with everyone, including myself, that the kittens were here temporarily until they moved on to be adopted. That sounds easy to say in practice.

What is a "foster fail?" A "foster fail" occurs when a cat's foster parent adopts the cat. The word "fail" in this context isn't necessarily negative. If the foster parent is ready and able to adopt the cat, it isn't a "fail." In this case, it's a success—a win/win. *{References: Websites: 1p}*

The kittens were now 13 weeks old. Wow—time had flown! Soon, I was leaving for a business conference, and my husband would join me. Our cat care provider wasn't available during that time, so I asked a friend, an ailurophile, to take care of Momma Cat and The Boys while we were gone. I thought it might be fun for her son, too, to play with the kittens. Luckily, they were available. They would be caring for six cats—our three grown cats in the back of the house and three in the front—Momma Cat and The Boys.

I specified I wanted her son to stay in the hallway with The Boys unless they were on the bed. Then, he could hang out with and pet the kittens if she was there with him. I didn't know how Momma Cat would do around children and didn't want him trying to play with her under the bed where she hid because she might feel threatened and scratch him.

My friend told me her son did a great job of playing with the kittens. The kittens appeared to have the zoomies[1] when playing with him. I was happy he got the time with them because it's fun for kids when given an opportunity to play with kittens.

When I returned from my trip, I found out Christina could only have one kitten where she would be living. Time was running out, and we needed to finalize Christina's plan to take her kitten. It was tough because I felt guilty separating the two brother kittens. On the positive side, I would still see Little Gray occasionally when I visited Christina. I was sure the kitten remaining at my house, Tux, wouldn't have a problem getting adopted. I would have a problem turning him over to be adopted because he was so cute, and I had become quite attached.

---

1. Sudden bursts of energy in which a cat typically runs back and forth. *{References: Websites: 1q}*

11

Where is Home?

L ittle Gray ended up not taking a trip across the country. I went alone to visit Christina while Little Gray remained at my house. Leading up to that trip, Christina and I had several more discussions. She decided this wasn't the right time to take on having a kitten. I knew it had been a hard decision for her to make. Ultimately, I felt like she had made the right decision for herself and the kitten.

When I returned from my trip, I worked on getting Momma Cat and The Boys adopted. The timing was important because it's easier to adopt out kittens than adult cats, so I wanted to do this before The Boys got much older.

I wished for Momma Cat and The Boys to be adopted together. I knew it was a big wish. If not fulfilled, then I would adopt out The Boys together since that appeared to be the next best option. Then, I would look for someone with cat experience to adopt Momma Cat.

She was now one of the most affectionate cats I had ever known—an absolute sweetheart! Whenever I came around her, she purred loudly, rubbing against my legs, and when I put my hand out, standing up to place her head into it. I could even hear her purr from across the room! However, it had taken months of building trust with her to get to where we were now. I also needed someone to adopt Momma Cat, who had the time and patience to build trust with her.

While chatting with Nadine, I mentioned my goal to adopt out Momma Cat and The Boys as a family by the end of the month. I needed to lighten my load because of some pressing issues. She asked, "Are you certain you want to give up Momma Cat?" Honestly, I wasn't sure. I thought it better for her to be adopted with The Boys since she'd be more comfortable having them there.

I had grown attached to Momma Cat. She was affectionate, playful, and often talked to me in her cat lingo. I had a lot of respect for her after watching how well she cared for her kittens. Still, keeping her with our three cats wasn't realistic, and I no longer considered putting her back outside because she wasn't feral. Living indoors made the most sense for Momma Cat and the community.

Before I answered Nadine's question, I would double-check with my husband. I knew he would support me either way. However, this needed to be more of a household discussion.

Even though it would be adding just one more cat, it would change the dynamics of our household cats. We would then have four female cats—our oldest cat is already a diva with the other two. I couldn't imagine our diva-like cat being happy with another cat, taking away some of the precious attention she received from her humans.

After talking more with my husband, we both agreed we wanted to go back to just having our three cats. Although we loved Momma Cat, and I had built a strong bond with her, we never intended to take on more cats. We had been working on simplifying our lives before Momma Cat and the kittens showed up. Although she was a sweetheart of a cat, she needed to be someone else's sweet cat. We were at capacity with our three cats, and they were tolerating The Littles Family.

Nadine said she would talk to her friends to see if someone might be interested in adopting at least The Boys and maybe Momma Cat, too. If they took all three, that would be great. If only The Boys were adopted, I would look for someone who could care for and love Momma Cat.

At this point, I guessed Momma Cat's age to be about one year old and the kittens' age to be about five and a half months old. All cats were healthy, spayed/neutered, and had up-to-date shots. Also, whoever adopted them could meet me, the person who had fostered them. Both times I adopted a set of kittens from the Humane Society, I was lucky to meet the people who fostered them. What fortunate timing! I got to hear some of the kittens' history.

After Nadine checked in with several friends about adopting The Littles Family or just The Boys, it became apparent that the timing wasn't good for anybody. I appreciated her for trying. She wanted to help this cat family stay together as much as possible.

I decided to hold off for another week and then check out a few other possibilities for private adoption. After that, if no one were available to adopt the kittens, I would consider checking into some public adoption options, where I'm sure they would have been quickly adopted. I still hoped to adopt all three together, so that's why I initially worked on private adoptions.

Nadine wished she could take The Littles Family herself. I wished it, too, because I knew her family would be the right family for the cats, especially Momma Cat. Unfortunately, the timing wasn't good for Nadine's family, either.

Two days later, I received a message from Nadine. Her family considered adopting The Littles Family and needed more time to discuss the situation. This time would help me mentally prepare for when they did go to their forever home, whether with Nadine's family, if it worked out, or someone else.

I was hoping this would work out. I would love for the Littles Family to live with Nadine's family. I knew they would love and take good care of The Littles Family.

Nadine's family planned to come over the next day. It would be a big win/win if they adopted The Littles Family.

The following day, Nadine told me her family looked forward to seeing The Littles Family that afternoon. Nadine's family had already decided to make The Littles Family part of their family.

I told my husband this was a win/win situation. Although I would miss The Littles Family, it warmed my heart to know they were going to this good family.

Before Nadine's family came over, I moved The Littles Family out of their usual space and into their other "play space" so her family could fully see them in action. Since Nadine's family was new to the Littles Family, there was a good chance The Littles Family would have run under the bed if left in their usual space.

Nadine's family interacted with The Boys for about an hour, petting and playing with them. Momma Cat was shy around them, so she went into the nearby bathroom and hid behind the toilet.

During this time, I prepared the cats' supplies to give to Nadine's family. I would provide them with the cat tower, toys, a clean litter box, litter, and wet and dry cat food. The food and litter primarily would serve as a transition—what The Littles Family was familiar with. To further transition them, Nadine's family would initially set them up in a small space, a bathroom, in their home. To help me to transition, it would be an open adoption. I could visit The Littles Family when I missed them. The open adoption was for Christina, too.

When it came time for Nadine's family to leave, I went to pick Momma Cat up to move her to the cat carrier, and she ran off and tried to hide. I felt sad about putting her in the carrier and saying "Goodbye," too. As my eyes filled with tears, I finally managed to get Momma Cat into the carrier. I didn't get to pet her before she left because I knew she would have attempted to escape the carrier if I tried. I saw her do something similar when I took her to the veterinarian.

The Boys were set to go in the other carrier. I watched as Nadine's family packed the two carriers containing the Littles Family into their car.

That was that. Nadine's family had become their new family. After five months, Momma Cat and The Boys were gone from my home, but not from my heart. I couldn't believe it and missed them already. I had become quite attached to them, much more than I expected. I had a tough time letting Momma Cat go because we had built up trust, and I loved her, too. In my heart, though, I knew letting her go to another family was the right thing to do.

On top of that, I was incredibly grateful to Nadine and her family for taking all three cats. These cats had more time together to bond, so it would have been harder, especially for Momma Cat, for them to go their separate ways. They could have adjusted, but how nice it was unnecessary to do so.

The Littles Family got a permanent home, and Nadine's family had a beautiful cat family to care for and love. Several people are in Nadine's household, so the cats will receive a lot of love.

Ironically, one of those people is Nadine's son, Ray, who had coached me by phone regarding Momma Cat when I thought she was feral.

Even though I knew The Littles Family went to a good family, it was still hard for me. As heartbreaking as it was to say "Goodbye" to Momma Cat and The Boys, I think this quote from the 19th century English poet, Alfred, Lord Tennyson, sums up my feelings, "Tis better to have loved and lost than never to have loved at all." Who says you can't apply poetry to cats, right?

The Next Big Adventure

The next day, I did a lot of post-kitten cleaning. While caring for the kittens was a lot of work, it also was fulfilling.

That night, Nadine and I exchanged texts. She sent me some beautiful pictures of Momma Cat and The Boys. They looked like they were settling in well in their new home, and I felt better already. I heard The Boys had been playing and exploring and then joined Momma Cat for a long nap under a side table. They were true "Mama's" boys.

Being able to go together was a gift for The Littles Family and would make their transition easier. Again, I really appreciated that Nadine's family made that possible.

At my house, we were back to just our three cats. As cute as the kittens were, I had come to appreciate our three cats more. We had raised them from kittens, and all had distinct and engaging personalities and were affectionate, playful lap cats. Calli, the moody calico, was happy to have my undivided attention and lap back. Occasionally, one of our cats walked around looking for something. I suspect they were looking for The Littles Family.

Over time, Nadine continued to share pictures of The Littles Family. They were looking cuter than ever. One fun picture was of Little Gray looking into the bathroom mirror at himself. He was intently looking at the "other" cat. He used to do that at my house, too. I wonder if he'll ever figure it out.

From the pictures, I could see that The Boys were relaxed in their new home. Momma Cat also looked comfortable in the home, and I heard she was being a sweet cat to Nadine's family. I suspected she would eventually become a lap cat who gives hugs.

The Boys, on the other hand, were still in their wild kitten stage. Nadine worked on minor kitten-proofing in her house for those two. I strongly felt that they would settle down more as they got older. My family had a pair of kittens twice over the years that we saw grow into adult cats. As kittens, they had so much energy, comparatively. Of course, adult cats can surprise us at times with their energy. At my house, our two 5-year-old sister cats tumble on the floor together and chase each other upstairs and downstairs like kittens.

When The Boys went after indoor plants at Nadine's house, her family quickly removed The Boys' access to the plants. Eating particular types of plants can make cats sick.

Protecting cats from plants and plants from cats: Keep cats away from toxic flowers and other plants. Cats often eat plants and can become sick or worse afterward. Some plants known to be toxic to cats are lilies, irises, poinsettias, and hyacinths. Before bringing plants into a cat's environment, research the plant's compatibility with cats. *{References: Books: 2, pgs.112-113}*

Speaking of health, the health history paperwork for The Littles Family was ready for Nadine, and the microchip needed to be updated with her information. I needed to put birthdates down for the kitties. I guessed The Boys were born about two weeks before I found them in my backyard. That was a more straightforward guess than with Momma Cat. Different vets who had examined her and given her vaccinations either placed her as a kitten herself or between 1-2 years old. I thought a fitting birthdate for Momma Cat would be the first day of autumn, the previous year, making her one year old. This autumn date matched the autumn colors in her fur.

With Nadine's latest batch of pictures, I commented on The Boys as beautiful kitties. Momma Cat, a beautiful cat herself, helped provide them with "cute kitty" genes. Little Gray's overall coloring was gorgeous, and the white coloring on Tux's paws matched perfectly together.

Beautiful Little Gray

Magnificent Tux

One adorable picture of The Boys was when they were lying down, hugging each other, showing brotherly love. Nadine mentioned they were sweet for a while, cuddling, and then Little Gray had to start wrestling with his brother.

World Kitten Wrestling

Also, I remembered something else funny about the kittens that I wanted to share with Nadine. That day, I put on my fuzzy slippers, and they reminded me of how much Little Gray loved it when I wore fuzzy socks. He would lie down on my feet and roll around. I suggested putting on some fuzzy socks if she wanted more kitty fun. Nadine told me she had already discovered Little Gray's love of all things fuzzy because he had the zoomies when he lay down on her fuzzy blanket.

Nadine noticed how photogenic Momma Cat and The Boys were. Momma Cat had such a beautiful, majestic look. It was nice that she was happy in her new home and no longer had a sad look in her eyes. I remember that look when she still lived outside.

She had gone through so many changes—being outside, being inside, and then moving to a different home. That was a lot of changes for her. Momma Cat was one very resilient cat!

Regal Momma Cat

During the five months I had Momma Cat and her five kittens, I went from having three cats to nine, then six, then back to three. It was easy to know that nine cats were too many for my family. However, when we were down to six cats, my and my daughter's love of cats kept us from thinking practically about the situation. I sometimes asked myself, "Does this qualify me as a crazy cat person?" Even if it did, I'm okay with that because sometimes we really step out of our comfort zone to help in a situation, and this was one of those times.

In life, we have to make choices based on time, money, and circumstances. As much as I loved The Littles Family, my family already had three cats. It was tough for me to say "Goodbye" to Momma Cat and her kitties, who had been part of my life, yet it was the right thing to do. It was quite a journey!

Reflecting on this beautiful cat journey, there are two cat families of three cats each, with humans who love them and include them as part of their family. It was a win/win/win when we consider the community since there are six fewer cats out there, no longer adding to the community cat population.

Finally, the best part of all—Momma Cat, Tux, and Little Gray's beautiful cat story continues—inside their forever home!

Looking for their next adventure

Afterword

Three wishes fulfilled (and without a genie's lamp.) This usually doesn't happen in life, especially in such a short period—five months. Two wishes occurred in the main part of the book—Christina's wish for a kitten and my wish for Momma Cat and The Boys to be adopted together. A third wish, mentioned in the Introduction, involved me volunteering to foster kittens someday. Little did I know the universe would fulfill that wish much sooner than expected and in a bigger way.

Initially, I was supposed to have the five kittens until they were eight weeks old. Then, they would go to a local animal welfare organization to be adopted out. Christina and her friend wanting to adopt The Boys meant I held on to those two longer. When those plans fell through, it gave me more time to spend with The Boys, and I became even more attached to them. My earlier plan to name the mother cat the generic name "Momma Cat" didn't work to keep me from becoming too attached to her either. I know how easy it is to get attached to our fur babies. They become family members.

How fortunate that the three cats went together to a family that understands this and knows how to love and care for them. I will forever be grateful to Nadine's family. I hear The Littles Family has been quite a gift for them, too.

The Boys have become bigger than their mother and are loving towards her, each other, and their human family. These boys continue to be as rambunctious as ever. Momma Cat is very loving. She purrs loudly, rubs up against legs, and talks to the humans more now. Who knows, this cat, which we thought was feral initially, may become a lap cat.

I have so much respect for Momma Cat (who, along with The Boys, have new names at their new home) because of how well she cared for her kittens. It was an amazing experience and some work for me to come along on their journey. I am happy to have had this opportunity. During this experience, I learned three big lessons:

- Finding kittens alone outside: Consider that the mother cat may temporarily be away getting food and water or checking out a safer place to move the kittens. It is best to monitor the situation before making a decision regarding the kittens.

- Weaning: Before adopting kittens, it's best if they are

already weaned.

- Feral cats: Not all community cats are feral.

Sage's support was immeasurable along the way, and she revealed that it was rewarding for her to help. Regarding Sage's help, it's fitting to refer back to Maya Angelou's words, "I did then what I knew how to do. Now that I know better, I do better." Sage empowered me throughout this journey to know better so I could do better to help these community cats.

Speaking of helping community cats, this leads to my second big motivation for writing this book (the first I disclosed in the Introduction)—I want more people to know about community cats and to help the effort to get them spayed or neutered. Bob Barker, the "Price is Right" game show host for 25 years, supported this important effort by ending each episode with these words: "Bob Barker, to remind you, help to control the pet population—have your pets spayed or neutered. Goodbye, everybody!"

Dear Readers, I wish for you to be inspired and feel more empowered by this beautiful cat story to help the beautiful cats in your community.

Acknowledgements

A special thank you to **my husband** for being so patient while I fostered six cats—Momma Cat and the five kittens—in one part of the house while we had our three indoor cats in another part of the house. Having nine cats inside one house really tests the "For better, for worse" part of one's wedding vows. I appreciated that you supported me while I worked things out with our four-legged house guests! You also listened and gave constructive feedback on the many read-throughs of parts of the book along the way. As I found out, writing my first book was quite the learning curve and <u>really</u> tough at times. Your suggestions were invaluable, wordsmithing exceptional, and your grounding support helped me when I needed encouragement the most. I love experiencing life's adventures with you. Thank you for everything!

Thank you to **Christina** for adding more joy, fun, and excitement to my life. This beautiful cat story began with your powerful kitten wish. You are truly one of my greatest wishes fulfilled—a daughter who became her own person and is lovely inside and out.

Thank you to my friend **Karen** for your support and feedback on my speeches over the years. These speeches involved writing and often storytelling—which was my training ground for writing this book. Also, you lent a much-needed listening ear throughout this cat journey.

Thank you to **Nadine** for caring so much about Momma Cat and The Boys and supporting them in having a home together. You and your family are heroes in my book.

Momma Cat and I thank **Ray** for sharing his cat knowledge with me. You helped to positively change the course of Momma Cat's life.

Thank you to **Sage** for Momma Cat and kitten coaching throughout this journey. Your support was immeasurable.

Thank you to **Tonya, Daria,** our **cat care provider**, and **other friends and family** who helped by giving advice or taking care of Momma Cat and the kittens in person.

Thank you to **Jane, Linda, Moira, Sondra,** and **other friends** for doing read-throughs and providing helpful suggestions for improvement.

Thank you to the **Fabulous Four on Fridays** for our engaging discussions. You helped me get out of my comfort zone to write this book.

Thank you to **Jerry** for your time and for sharing insights as an experienced author with me, a new author.

Thank you to **Angie Alaya** for the wonderful book cover design, which made the beautiful kitten on the front cover come alive.

Thank you to **the Humane Society of Silicon Valley volunteers** who cared for and fostered our household cats when they were kittens. These kittens became a part of our family and grew into beautiful cats. How kittens are socialized makes a difference as they grow up, and seeing that with my cats served as a reminder when I was socializing Momma Cat and the kittens.

References

Books

1. Hattori, Dr. Yuki. *What Cats Want: An illustrated guide for truly understanding your cat*. London, United Kingdom: Bloomsbury Publishing, 2020.

2. Pilbeam, Rosie. *The Complete Book of Cats*. London, United Kingdom: Anness Publishing Limited, 2021.

Websites

(NOTE: The URLs listed below were accurate as of the publishing date. See the Copyright page for more details.)

1. **catster**

   a. Billingsley, Brooke. "How Many Kittens Can a Cat Have? Vet Verified Facts & FAQ." *catster*, 20 Sep. 2024, **https://www.catster.com/cat-health-care/how-many-kittens-can-a-cat-have/**.

   b. Dickson, Patricia. "How Often Will a Feral Cat Move Her Kittens? Vet Verified Facts & FAQ." *catster*, 26 Sep. 2024, **https://www.catster.com/cat-behavior/how-often-will-a-feral-cat-move-her-kittens/**.

   c. Dugal, Genevieve. "Why Does An Adult Cat Go Limp When You Grab Their Scruff? Vet-Verified Reasons & FAQ." *catster*, 25 Sep. 2024, **https://www.catster.com/lifestyle/why-does-an-adult-cat-go-limp-when-you-grab-their-scruff/**.

   d. Morgan, Annaliese. "When Do Cats Stop Growing & Reach Their Full Size? Vet Verified Facts & FAQ." *catster*, 28 Sep. 2024, **https://www.catster.com/cat-health-care/when-do-cats-stop-growing/**.

e. Adams, Christian. "When Is Kitten Season? Quick Vet-Reviewed Facts." *catster*, 2 Oct. 2024, **https://www.catster.com/lifestyle/wh en-is-kitten-season/**.

f. Kim, Jessica. "Cat Reproduction & Mating: Vet-Approved Facts & Explanation." *catster*, 4 Oct. 2024, **https://www.catster.com/cat-heal th-care/cat-reproduction-and-mating/**.

g. Jackson, Matt. "14 Cat Overpopulation Statistics (2024 Update)." *catster*, 6 Sep. 2024, **https://www.catster.com/statistics/cat -overpopulation-statistics/**.

h. Kim, Jessica. "How to Bottle Feed a Kitten: Vet-Approved Tips & Feeding Chart (With Video)." *catster*, 3 Oct. 2024, **https://www.catster.com/cat-health-ca re/how-to-bottle-feed-a-kitten/**.

i. Chandley, Dr. Emma. "Do Female Cats Have Periods? Heat Cycle Explained (Vet Answer)." *catster*, 13 Sep. 2024, **https://www.catster.com/a sk-the-vet/do-female-cats-have-periods/**.

j. Luther, Lorre. "Can a Litter of Kittens Have Different Fathers? Vet-Verified Facts & FAQ." *catster*, 20 Sep. 2024, **https://www.catster.com/cat-health-care/can -a-litter-of-kittens-have-different-fathers/**.

k. Adams, Christian. "Why Is My Cat Purring After Giving Birth? 7 Vet-Reviewed Reasons." *catster*, 9 Sep. 2024, **https://www.catster.com/cat-health-care/why-is-cat-purring-after-giving-birth/**.

l. Adams, Christian. "How to Introduce a Kitten to a Cat: 10 Vet-Approved Tips." *catster*, 17 Sep. 2024, **https://www.catster.com/lifestyle/how-to-introduce-a-kitten-to-a-cat/**.

m. Adams, Christian. "Pellet Litter vs Clumping: Our 2024 Comparison, Pros & Cons." *catster*, 30 Aug. 2024, **https://www.catster.com/lifestyle/pellet-litter-vs-clumping/**.

n. Kanowski, Dr. Karyn. "Feline Leukemia (FeLV) Vaccines for Cats: A Complete Guide (Vet Answer)." *catster*, 26 Sep. 2024, **https://www.catster.com/ask-the-vet/feline-leukemia-felv-vaccines-for-cats/**.

o. Devine, Dr. Samantha. "FIV in Cats (Feline Immunodeficiency Virus): Vet Explained Causes, Signs & Care." *catster*, 4 Oct. 2024, **https://www.catster.com/ask-the-vet/fiv-in-cats/**.

p. Gray, Elizabeth. "Cat Fostering: 8 Vet-Approved Reasons You Should Consider It." *catster*, 5 Sep. 2024, **https://www.catster.com/cat-behavior/cat-fostering/**.

q. Woodnutt, Dr. Joanna. "Cat Zoomies: What Are They & When to Worry? (Vet Answer)." *catster*, 18 Sep. 2024, **https://www.catster.com/ask-t he-vet/cat-zoomies/**.

r. Adams, Christian. "Did Cleopatra Have Cats? Egyptian Cat History Explained."
catster,   2   Aug.   2024, **https://www.catster.com/lifestyle/did-cleopa tra-have-cats/#:~:text=While%20contempor ary%20records%20don't,support%20or%20d eny%20these%20claims.**.

s. catster Editorial Staff. "Betty White Talks to the Cat's Meow." *catster*, 12 July 2024, **https://www.catster.com/lifestyle/bet ty-white-talks-to-the-cats-meow/**.

t. Uys, Crystal. "Exploring the Cats of the Rich & Famous: 20 Celebrity Kitties." *catster*, 25 Sep. 2024, **https://www.catster.com/lifestyle/exp loring-the-cats-of-the-rich-and-famous/**.

2. **Guinness Book of World Records**

a. "Largest Litter of Domestic Cats." *Guinness Book of   World   Records*, **https://www.guinnessworldrecords.com/wo rld-records/largest-litter-domestic-cat**. Accessed 3 Sep. 2024.

b. "Oldest Cat Ever." *Guinness Book of World Records*, **https://www.guinnessworldrecords .com/world-records/oldest-cat-ever**. Accessed 16 Sep. 2024.

3. **Alley Cat Allies**

a. "The Cat Socialization Continuum: A Guide to Interactions Between Cats and Humans." *Alley Cat Allies*, **https://www.alleycat.org/resou rces/cat-socialization-continuum-guide/**. Accessed 4 Sep. 2024.

b. So You've Decided to TNR." *Alley Cat Allies*, **https://www.alleycat.org/community-c at-care/so-youve-decided-to-tnr/**. Accessed 4 Sep. 2024.

c. "TNR Scenarios: Nursing Mother Cat." *Alley Cat Allies*, **https://www.alleycat.org/community-cat-car e/tnr-scenarios-nursing-mother-cat/**. Accessed 4 Sep. 2024.

d. "Special Considerations and Equipment Necessary for Handling a Feral Cat." *Alley Cat Allies*, **https://www.alleycat.org/resources/special-c onsiderations-and-equipment-necessary-for -handling-a-feral-cat/**. Accessed 4 Sep. 2024.

e. "Cat Identification Guide." *Alley Cat Allies*, **https://www.alleycat.org/resources/cat-identification-guide/**. Accessed 4 Sep. 2024.

4. Kitten Lady

a. Shaw, Hannah. "Determining a Kitten's Age." *Kitten Lady*, **http://www.kittenlady.org/age**. Accessed 3 Sep. 2024.

b. Shaw, Hannah. "How to Care For a Nursing Mama & Her Babies." *Kitten Lady*, **https://www.kittenlady.org/mama?rq=nursing**. Accessed 3 Sep. 2024.

c. Shaw, Hannah. "Weaning Kittens." *Kitten Lady*, **https://kittenlady.org/weaning**. Accessed 3 Sep. 2024.

d. Shaw, Hannah. "Helping Feral Kittens Become Friendly." *Kitten Lady*, **https://www.kittenlady.org/feral**. Accessed 3 Sep. 2024.

5. San Jose Animal Care Center

a. "Kittens." *San Jose Animal Care Center*, **https://www.sanjoseca.gov/your-government/departments-offices/animal-care-services/services/community-cats-and-tnr/kittens**. Accessed 5 Sep. 2024.

6. Merriam-Webster Online Dictionary

a. "nest." *Merriam-Webster Online Dictionary*, **https://www.merriam-webster.com/dictionary/nest**. Accessed 8 Sep. 2024.

b. "queen." *Merriam-Webster Online Dictionary*, **https://www.merriam-webster.com/dictionary/queen**. Accessed 8 Sep. 2024.

c. "tom." *Merriam-Webster Online Dictionary*, **https://www.merriam-webster.com/dictionary/tom**. Accessed 8 Sep. 2024.

d. "capacity." *Merriam-Webster Online Dictionary*, **https://www.merriam-webster.com/dictionary/capacity**. Accessed 8 Sep. 2024.

e. "gestation." *Merriam-Webster Online Dictionary*, **https://www.merriam-webster.com/dictionary/gestation**. Accessed 29 Sep. 2024.

f. "ailurophile." *Merriam-Webster Online Dictionary*, **https://www.merriam-webster.com/dictionary/ailurophile**. Accessed 8 Sep. 2024.

7. **Bay Area Cats**

a. "Trap-Neuter-Return(TNR) Workshop." *Bay Area Cats*, **https://bayareacats.org/resources/workshop.pdf**. Accessed 3 Sep. 2024.

8. **Royal Museums Greenwich**

a. "Oscar, cat from the German battleship 'Bismarck'." *Royal Museums Greenwich*, **https://www.rmg.co.uk/collections/objects/rmgc-object-203480**. Accessed 17 Sep. 2024.

9. **Encyclopaedia Britannica**

a. Carroll, K. and René Ostberg. "9 (Lives of) Famous Cat Lovers." *Britannica*, 11 June 2024, **https://www.britannica.com/topic/9-Lives-of-Famous-Cat-Lovers**.

10. **Smithsonian Magazine**

a. Oster, Lauren. "A Colorful History of Cats in the White House." *Smithsonian Magazine*, 11 Feb. 2022, **https://www.smithsonianmag.com/history/a-colorful-history-of-cats-in-the-white-house-180979561/**.

b. Eschner, Kat. "Mark Twain Liked Cats Better Than People." *Smithsonian Magazine*, 16 Oct. 2017, **https://www.smithsonianmag.com/smart-news/mark-twain-liked-cats-better-people-180965265/**.

11. **The Ernest Hemingway Home and Museum**

a. "Our Cats." *The Ernest Hemingway Home and Museum*, **https://www.hemingwayhome.com/our-cats**. Accessed 17 Sep. 2024.

12. **Discover Museum**

a. George, Stephen. "Five Cats Who Owned Famous Scientists." *Discover Magazine*, 29 Aug. 2 0 2 2 , **https://www.discovermagazine.com/the-sciences/5-cats-who-owned-famous-scientists**.

13. **BBC**

a. "Who was the real Florence Nightingale?" *BBC*, **https://www.bbc.co.uk/programmes/articles/1Zk9scdx1WCLDjjV5LKdz8R/who-was-the-real-florence-nightingale**. Accessed 18 Sep. 2024.

14. **Winston Churchill**

a. "Churchill and Cats." *Winston Churchill*, **https://winstonchurchill.org/churchill-central/storyelement/churchill-and-cats/**. Accessed 18 Sep. 2024.

Appendix A: Brief History of Cats

Cats' history probably dates back to the wild cats of over 35 million years ago. Cat skeletons discovered in the Middle East provided evidence of cats living amongst humans, going back about 9,000 years. Cats were most likely not domesticated at that time. The most similar living situation to modern times between humans and cats can be traced back to Egypt about 3,500 years ago.

When humans moved to an agricultural way of life, cats became more like domestic companions. There was a mutually beneficial relationship between cats and humans. Cats took care of the rodent population for the humans, and the humans fed the cats.

Most of today's domestic cats were likely ancestors of the African wild cat (Felis sylvestris libyca). Cats' genetic makeup is very similar to that of tigers.

Today, cats are the world's second most popular domestic pets, dogs being the first. When considering numbers, though, counting wild and domestic together worldwide, cats outnumber dogs.[1]

Some famous cats in history and popular culture:

- **Cat in the Hat**—the main character in the book *The Cat in the Hat* by Dr. Seuss (Theodor Seuss Geisel)

- **Cheshire Cat**—character in the book *Alice's Adventures in Wonderland* by Lewis Carroll

- **Creme Puff**—oldest cat ever (38 years, 3 days) *{References: Websites: 2b}*

- **Garfield**—comic strip character (created by Jim Davis)

---

1. *{References: Books:2, pgs. 6-7, 12- 15}*

- **Heathcliff**—comic strip character (created by George Gately and currently written by Peter Gallagher)

- **Hello Kitty**—Japanese cartoon character (created by Yuko Shimizu, currently designed by Yuko Yamaguchi, and owned by the Japanese company Sanrio)

- **Morris the Cat**—spokescat for the 9Lives brand cat food

- **Mr. Mistoffelees**—character in T.S. Eliot's poetry book, *Old Possum's Book of Practical Cats* (Andrew Lloyd Webber's musical "Cats" based on this)

- **Puss in Boots**—character in "Puss in Boots" fairy tale by Charles Perrault

- **Solomon**—the character Blofeld's cat in the James Bond movie franchise

- **Sylvester**—a cartoon character paired with the bird Tweety Pie (created by Friz Freleng for Looney Tunes and Merrie Melodies cartoon shows at Warner Brothers Studios)

- **Tom**—a cartoon character paired with Jerry (a mouse) in "Tom and Jerry" cartoons (created by William Hanna and Joseph Barbera for Metro-Goldwyn-Mayer (MGM) Studios)

- **"Unsinkable Sam" (known as Oscar/Oskar, orig-**

inally)—the legendary cat purported to have survived despite ships he was on being torpedoed during WWII *{References: Websites: 8a}*

Some Famous Cat-lovers:

- **Cleopatra**—ancient Egyptian queen (speculated to have had a cat and is listed here to represent the ancient Egyptians' reverence for cats) *{References: Websites: 1r}*

- **Catherine the Great**—Empress of Russia who founded the Hermitage Museum in St. Petersburg, Russia, in the 1700s, and had cats brought to the museum as "guardians of the galleries" to reduce the rodent population *{References: Websites: 9a}*

- **Florence Nightingale**—a nurse who helped bring about positive changes to the nursing industry in England during the 1800s and adopted at least 60 cats during her lifetime *{References: Websites: 13a}*

- **Abraham Lincoln**—the 16th U.S. President and the first U.S. President to have cats as pets in the White House *{References: Websites: 10a}*

- **Mark Twain**—a 20th-century American author who had 19 cats at one time *{References: Websites: 10b}*

- **Winston Churchill**—British Prime Minister in the 1940's (during WWII) who had several cats, with

Jock being his favorite *{References: Websites: 14a}*

- **Albert Einstein**—a 20th-century theoretical physicist who had a cat named Tiger *{References: Websites: 12a}*

- **Ernest Hemingway**—a 20th-century American author who kept many cats (some polydactyl[2]) in his home in Key West, Florida *{References: Websites: 11a}*

- **Betty White**—an American actress and comedian who loved cats and supported several animal organizations during her lifetime, especially the Morris Animal Foundation *{References: Websites: 1s}*

- **Robert Downey Jr.**—an American actor who loves his cats Montgomery and Dartanian *{References: Websites: 1t}*

- **Taylor Swift**—an American singer-songwriter who has three cats, and one of them, Benjamin Button, appeared with her on a Time Magazine 2023 Person of the Year cover *{References: Websites: 9a}*

---

2. *(in regards to cats) having an extra toe or toes {References: Websites: 3e}*

Appendix B: Author's History with Cats

As a toddler, I loved taking our patient family cat, Fluffy, for a spin in my stroller. He kept jumping in, so he must have liked my driving.

As a kindergartener, I met my first kittens. My mother and I walked two blocks to my godmother's house to see her cat with the four kittens. I remember how cute the kittens were, running around her living room. They were probably about five weeks old at the time. This experience further cemented my love for cats.

Eventually, Fluffy passed away, and a grayish-brown tabby, Tigger, joined our family. He became my parents' cat and companion when their kids were grown and out on their own.

At my first apartment after college, a beautiful tortoiseshell cat appeared one day in the courtyard near my apartment. Later, I discovered that a family had left this cat when they moved.

This tortoiseshell cat started coming up to me. I felt bad—the cat looked thin—so I gave her food. She then came to my door in the early morning, meowing. I took her inside, fed her, and called her Calli (I didn't know then that she was a tortoiseshell. I thought she was a calico cat.) You know what happens next—Calli adopted me! She was around one year old at the time.

Calli lived to be 19. After her passing, I took a break from having cats because I missed her terribly. A few years later, when my daughter was in preschool, I took her every so often to visit the cats at the Humane Society. We helped to give the cats love and attention.

When my daughter was nine years old, a nice lady from Project Cornerstone—a community initiative of the YMCA of Silicon Valley—encouraged me to consider getting my daughter a cat as a companion since she didn't have siblings. Due to my past experience with Calli when I was single and lived alone—she seemed so lonely when I was away at work—my husband and I decided to let our daughter adopt two cats to keep each other company when we were away. We went to a Humane Society Satellite Adoption Center inside a Petco and adopted two cats—a brother and a sister.

My daughter and I apparently inherited my family of origin's habit of renaming our animals after beloved pets that have passed (I think we got to Fluffy the Third). We named the female cat Calli (the second, after my cat Calli, the first.) She was really a calico cat this time. Her brother, Mr. Pumpkin, fit his name perfectly. We enjoyed six years of fun times with Mr. Pumpkin. When he passed, we adopted two more cats, sisters, from the same Humane Society Satellite Adoption Center as before. These cat sisters are mentioned in *A Beautiful Cat Story: What Happened After the First Meow.*

Donations to the Cat Cause

10% of this book's profits will be donated to nonprofit animal welfare organizations, such as those listed below.

- Alley Cat Allies—https://www.alleycat.org/

- Bay Area Cats—https://bayareacats.org/donate

- Humane Society of Silicon Valley— https://www.hssv.org/

- Orphan Kitten Club (Kitten Lady Hannah Shaw's Nonprofit)—https://orphankittenclub.org/donate/

- San Jose Animal Care Center—https://www.sanjoseca.gov/your-government/departments-offices/animal-care-services/ways-to-give/donate/

About the Author

Becky Divinski grew up with cats in Torrance, California. She enjoys hiking, traveling (noticing cats during her journeys), and eating a variety of foods (a favorite of her cats.) In her work as a parent and teacher educator (she is a Certified Positive Discipline Lead Trainer), Becky became familiar with a German word, Gemeinschaftsgefühl, a word often used by 19th-century Viennese psychotherapist Alfred Adler, which means "social interest; a sense of community." She values this concept, whether dealing with people or our animal friends.

Becky's history with cats (Appendix B) and her recent big adventure led her to share the story and wisdom gained from this experience. *A Beautiful Cat Story: What Happened After the First Meow* is Becky's first book.

www.ingramcontent.com/pod-product-compliance
Lightning Source LLC
Chambersburg PA
CBHW071755120626
46550CB00002B/797